The
Yorkshire
Terrier

An Owner's Guide To

A HAPPY HEALTHY PET

Howell Book House

Wiley Publishing, Inc.

For general information on our other products and services, please contact our Customer Care Department within the U.S. at 800-762-2974, outside the U.S. at 317-572-3993 or fax 317-572-4002.

Wiley also publishes its books in a variety of electronic formats. Some content that appears in print may not be available in electronic books.

Library of Congress Cataloging-in-Publication data

Lane, Marion.

The Yorkshire terrier: an owner's guide to a happy, healthy pet/by Marion Lane.

p.cm.

ISBN 0-87605-477-7

1. Yorkshire terriers. I. Title.
SF429.Y6L36   1996, 2001
636.7'6—dc20   96-3952
                      CIP

Manufactured in the United States of America
10   9

Second Edition

Series Director: Kira Sexton
Book design: Michele Laseau
Cover design: Mike Freeland
Photography Editor: Richard Fox
Illustration: Jeff Yesh
Photography:
  Front and back cover photos supplied by Jeannie Harrison/Close Encounters of the Furry Kind
  Joan Balzarini: 96
  Mary Bloom: 9, 21, 40, 96, 136, 145
  Paulette Braun/Pets by Paulette: 5, 11, 24, 32, 38, 61, 96
  Buckinghamhill American Cocker Spaniels: 148
  Sian Cox: 134
  Dr. Ian Dunbar: 98, 101, 102, 111, 116, 117, 122, 123, 127
  Marion Lane: 26
  Carl Lindemauer: 19
  Dan Lyons: 96
  Scott McKiernan/Zuma: 8, 26, 50, 51, 52, 53, 55, 59, 134
  Cathy Merrithew: 129
  Liz Palika: 133
  Cheryl Primeau: 20
  Susan Rezy: 23, 39, 46, 96[nd]97, 136, 145
  Judith Strom: 37, 92, 96, 107, 110, 128, 130, 135, 137, 139, 140, 144, 149, 150
  Toni Tucker: 10
  Jean Wentworth: 34
  Kerrin Winter/Dale Churchill: 12, 15, 27, 35, 42, 48, 54, 66, 96, 97
  Photo on page 19 courtesy of Barbara Switzer
Page creation by: Wiley Indianapolis Composition Services

Contents

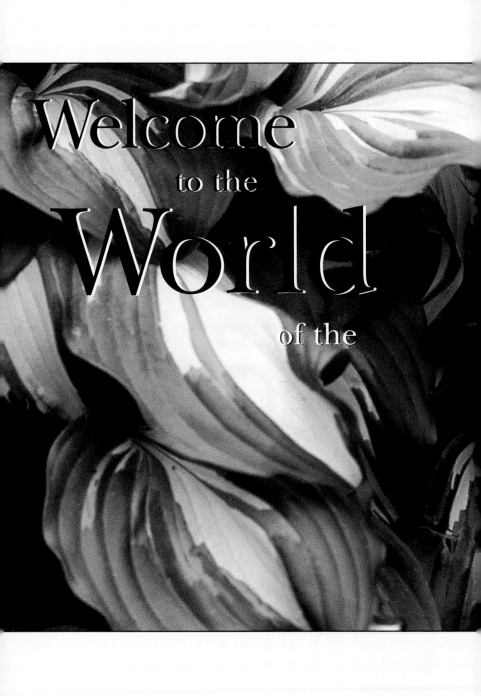

Welcome
to the
World
of the

part one

Yorkshire Terrier

External Features of the Yorkshire Terrier

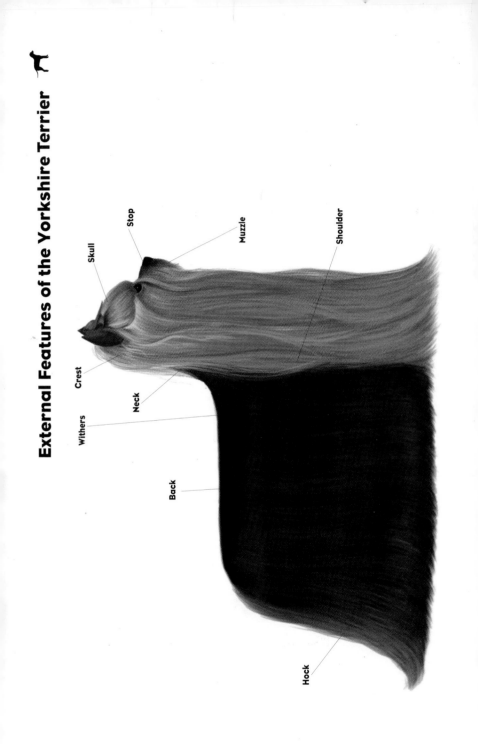

chapter 1

What

Is a
Yorkshire
Terrier?

The first time I heard of a Yorkshire Terrier was in 1978 when my boyfriend, Bill, decided that a Yorkie was what he wanted to give me for my birthday. Bill's friend, Rick, had a male Yorkie named Kong, and Bill was quite smitten with Kong—as smitten as any man of the seventies, who wanted to maintain his dignity, could honestly admit. Fortunately, Bill  knew that no one should surprise anyone with a dog, and he wisely wanted me to pick out my own puppy. In my heart, of course, I knew that Bill wanted this puppy as much for himself as for me, but I didn't mind. I happily threw myself into the project of researching the Yorkshire Terrier.

Always big on "book learnin'," the first thing I did was buy two Yorkshire Terrier breed books. The first was more of an illustrated booklet, and I honestly don't know if I did much more than drool over the pictures. It was only later when I saw my first Yorkie in the flesh that I realized the glamorous pictures had given me a false impression of this energetic little dog. The second book was a substantial but slow-going study of the Yorkshire, more suited to Yorkie historians, breeders and serious fanciers than to first-time owners. Only after I'd lived with a Yorkie for several years did I go back and take another look at these two books. Neither one had prepared me for either the challenges or the special joys of living with this breed. That's why every word of this book was written with that memory in mind.

General Appearance and the Yorkie Standard

Yorkie! The very name suggests something tiny, cute and perky, and the Yorkshire Terrier is certainly all of these things. As a well-established purebred dog, the Yorkie's unique physical aspects, or "type," as well as its character traits, are spelled out in a document called the Breed Standard. If you're anything like I was when I got my Yorkie, you probably think show dogs and dog shows are weird, and don't have a clue what this "standard" thing has to do with the puppy you're about to get for a companion. As it turns out, quite a lot!

The official standard, written by a group of breeders and fanciers known collectively as the Yorkshire Terrier Club of America, and approved by the American Kennel Club, is a kind of blueprint for breeders and judges. The standard ensures that none of the historically important features that characterize the Yorkshire Terrier will be lost in future generations. A puppy doesn't have to meet the standard in every way to make a suitable pet. On the other hand, if it's those things that make a Yorkie different from any other dog, it stands to reason that you'd want a puppy whose breeder had that in mind when they set out to create the magical creature who's coming to live at your house.

So how does the standard describe a Yorkshire Terrier? Fairly briefly. Since it's relatively short, the whole of it is printed here. I've broken it up into sections, with short comments about what each section means to me and you.

General Appearance *That of a long-haired Toy terrier whose blue and tan coat is parted on the face and from the base of the skull to the end of the tail and hangs evenly and quite straight down each side of body. The body is neat, compact and well proportioned. The dog's high head carriage and confident manner should give the appearance of vigor and self-importance.*

Comment on General Appearance: While the Yorkie's size, coat and color surely are its most unique physical characteristics, it's the terrier in the Yorkie that gives it its "Hey you!" attitude. Those of us who love Yorkies, love the complete package: tiny size, glossy good looks, keen intelligence and big-dog outlook on life.

Head *Small and rather flat on top, the skull not too prominent or round, the muzzle not too long, with the bite neither undershot nor overshot and teeth sound. Either scissors bite or level bite is acceptable. The nose is black. Eyes are medium in size and not too prominent; dark in color and sparkling with a sharp, intelligent expression. Eye rims are dark. Ears are small, V-shaped, carried erect and set not too far apart.*

Body *Well proportioned and very compact. The back is rather short, the back line level, with height at shoulder the same as at the rump.*

WHAT IS A BREED STANDARD?

A breed standard—a detailed description of an individual breed—is meant to portray the *ideal* specimen of that breed. This includes ideal structure, temperament, gait, type—all aspects of the dog. Because the standard describes an ideal specimen, it isn't based on any particular dog. It is a concept against which judges compare actual dogs and breeders strive to produce dogs. At a dog show, the dog that wins is the one that comes closest, in the judge's opinion, to the standard for its breed. Breed standards are written by the breed parent clubs, the national organizations formed to oversee the well-being of the breed. They are voted on and approved by the members of the parent clubs.

Legs and Feet   *Forelegs should be straight, elbows neither in nor out. Hind legs straight when viewed from behind, but stifles are moderately bent when viewed from the sides. Feet are round with black toenails. Dewclaws, if any, are generally removed from the hind legs. Dewclaws on the forelegs may be removed.*

Tail   *Docked to a medium length and carried slightly higher than the level of the back.*

Weight   *Must not exceed seven pounds.*

In dog shows, Yorkies are judged for their adherence to the breed standard.

Comment on Head, Body, Legs and Feet, Tail and Weight: If the human eye is pleased by balance and symmetry, the Yorkie is a sight for sore eyes indeed. The small head is in proportion with the compact body; the little prick ears on one end complement the docked tail on the other. With the whole package draped in steel-blue silk, the Yorkie looks like it belongs on the knee of a monarch.

Looks can be deceiving, and the term "toy" should not be taken literally. The Yorkie is a "for real" dog. If you treat your Duke of York like a toy, you may end up with a spoiled, even snappy, seven-pound tyrant (sometimes called the "Yorkshire Terrorist"). You will also deprive yourself of the joy of experiencing firsthand the Duke's legendary charm and "cheek."

The standard states that the Yorkie is compact and well proportioned. Underneath its very long coat, its crowning glory, the Yorkie's body is athletic and sturdy, designed for a long, active life. Important physical features are its short, level back (hips and shoulders are the same height) and its straight legs with moderately bent stifles (knees). The Yorkie also has a moderately long neck (important for carrying the head high) and enough forechest (the part that sticks out in front of the legs when viewed from the side) to house a good set of lungs for stamina. When trotting along on a loose lead, the Yorkie has a free, jaunty gait, with both head and tail held high. In the Yorkie, small does not mean frail or fragile.

This dog's "nose-to-nose" boldness is typical of Yorkie personality.

It's important for all Yorkies, whether show or companion quality, to have these basic physical features. Along with health and conditioning, it's a dog's underlying structure that determines the kinds of activities, or lifestyle, it can engage in. In the Yorkie's case, this includes at the very least long walks, preferably where there are squirrels to chase, a brisk game of catch in the backyard and a spirited session of "tug" in the living room. But it can also include organized all-weather dog sports such as obedience, tracking and agility (see Chapter 9)—which many owners think are too rigorous for small dogs. This is nonsense. A well-built Yorkie is able to do just about anything that a larger dog can do, simply on a "shorter" scale.

In perfect balance with the Yorkie's rugged little frame is his tough little spirit. The confident manner mentioned in the standard is as much a part of the Yorkshire Terrier as are its size and coat; the Yorkie's bearing must clearly convey that this is a vigorous small dog of considerable importance. But when you're ankle-high on the leg of the average human, how do you get that message across? With a look. And the physical features that do the most to make up the typical look of the Yorkie are his eyes and ears.

Yorkie eyes are dark, and they sparkle with intelligence; his small, erect and mobile ears are like radar dishes that telegraph the Yorkie's lively interest in everything around him. Although the ears are tipped over in very young puppies, they should stand erect by the time the dog is about three months old; the Yorkie without fully erect ears will never have typical Yorkie expression. Overall, the expression of the breed is alert, inquisitive and self-confident.

This Yorkie has the bright eyes and perky ears of a spirited and confident little dog.

Coat   *Quality, texture and quantity of coat are of prime importance. Hair is glossy, fine and silky in texture. Coat on the body is moderately long and perfectly straight (not wavy). It may be trimmed to floor length to give ease of movement and a neater appearance, if desired. The fall on the head is long, tied with one bow in center of head or parted in the middle and tied with two bows. Hair on muzzle is very long. Hair should be trimmed short on tops of ears and may be trimmed on feet to give them a neat appearance.*

10

Colors   *Puppies are born black and tan and are normally darker in body color, showing an intermingling of black hair in the tan until they are matured. Color of hair on body and richness of tan on head and legs are of prime importance in adult dogs, to which the following color requirements apply:*

BLUE: Is a dark steel-blue, not a silver-blue and not mingled with fawn, bronzy or black hairs.

TAN: All tan hair is darker at the roots than in the middle, shading to still lighter tan at the tips. There should be no sooty or black hair intermingled with any of the tan.

The long and shiny coat of a well-bred Yorkie gives the dog a luxurious appearance.

Color on Body   *The blue extends over the body from back of neck to root of tail. Hair on tail is a darker blue, especially at end of tail.*

Headfall   *A rich golden tan, deeper in color at sides of head, at ear roots and on the muzzle, with ears a deep rich tan. Tan color should not extend down on back of neck.*

Chest and Legs   *A bright, rich tan, not extending above the elbow on the forelegs nor above the stifle on the hind legs.*

Comment on Coat and Colors: When I first read the Yorkie breed standard, I had not yet seen a real live Yorkie. I wondered how anyone could get so worked up over a few dark hairs mixed in with the tan ones or care so much whether the blue looked like steel rather than silver. It all seemed kind of absurd. Clearly a

Yorkie whose coat color, length or texture was "off" was no less desirable as a pet! Then a long-time Yorkie fancier pointed out that the standard has changed very little since it was written in 1912. He asked me this: "How many car models, hair styles, hem lengths, dance steps and music crazes have come and gone in the same eighty-odd years?" The point is that if breeders didn't hold to an exacting standard with regard to coat, it wouldn't be long before the Yorkie lost his distinctive look. And isn't that what drew you and me to Yorkies in the first place?

While these dogs may not be "show quality" in appearance, their energy and interest still make them wonderful, happy pets.

Companion or Show Quality?

I bought my Yorkie from an Englishwoman named Joan who worked for the United Nations. The puppy was one of a litter of two females. I chose the puppy that was most daring and outgoing. Joan had named her Mary, but I had already decided to call her Lilli. Then Bill began to call her The Wee, and that stuck.

In my pride and prejudice, I thought The Wee would turn out to be a show dog. It was clear she was not bred from show lines, and my Yorkie breed book (the serious one) stated flatly that no silk purses will come from sow's ears where Yorkshire Terriers are concerned. Still, by the time she was six months old, the change in The Wee's appearance was so dramatic that I just knew she was going to be the exception to the rule. Then, in February, I went to the Westminster Dog Show at Madison Square Garden. It took only one good look to see that there was no way The Wee's coat was ever going to grow into the kind, color, texture or amount of a show dog's. In time I was able to see that she had just as many faults in other areas. Nonetheless, she was unmistakably a Yorkie, and unmistakably a Toy terrier. In terms of confidence, vigor and self-importance, she not only met but exceeded the standard.

In simplest terms, the difference between "show" quality and "companion" quality Yorkies is the extent to which they meet the standard. Still, the range of companion or "pet" quality Yorkies is extremely broad. It covers everything from a well-bred puppy with too many dark hairs in its tan to be a show dog, to the sentimental litter out of Aunt Sally's Freddy and her next-door neighbor's Maxine. But since it is the official standard that describes the ideal Yorkshire terrier, and it is only *because* of the standard that the Yorkshire Terrier type has survived to this day, I believe that the breeding of Yorkies should be left to those

THE AMERICAN KENNEL CLUB

Familiarly referred to as "the AKC," the American Kennel Club is a nonprofit organization devoted to the advancement of purebred dogs. The AKC maintains a registry of recognized breeds and adopts and enforces rules for dog events including shows, obedience trials, field trials, hunting tests, lure coursing, herding, earthdog trials, agility and the Canine Good Citizen program. It is a club of clubs, established in 1884 and composed, today, of over 500 autonomous dog clubs throughout the United States. Each club is represented by a delegate; the delegates make up the legislative body of the AKC, voting on rules and electing directors. The American Kennel Club maintains the Stud Book, the record of every dog ever registered with the AKC, and publishes a variety of materials on purebred dogs, including a monthly magazine, books and numerous educational pamphlets. For more information, contact the AKC at the address listed in Chapter 13, "Resources," and look for the names of their publications in Chapter 12, "Recommended Reading."

who follow the standard. That means that only a small percentage of the roughly 38,000 Yorkies registered by the AKC each year are suitable to be show (and breeding) stock. But, happily, every single one of them is suitable to be the world's best companion to its owner!

chapter 2

The Yorkshire Terrier's Ancestry

If the only Yorkshire Terriers you ever saw were show dogs in full coat and bow-tied topknots, you'd have a hard time imagining how on earth—and why—such a creature had come into existence. There's no question that today's Yorkie is first and foremost a companion dog. Although all dogs are willing and able to be someone's true-blue pal, few if any breeds were deliberately developed for that reason. If you go far enough back in the history of any pure breed of dogs, you're bound to discover an original utilitarian purpose. The Yorkshire Terrier is no exception.

Dog Breeding—Then

In nature, dogs do not vary widely. In different parts of the world, a few basic types evolved from the wolf, in keeping with local climate

14

and terrain. Virtually all of the exaggerated physical characteristics (such as very large or very small size; great coat length or density; and structural extremes such as large heads, flat faces, pendulous ears and elongated bodies) were selected for by man to enhance the dog's usefulness in some way. Likewise, when locally available dogs showed special ability or enthusiasm for specific tasks, people naturally bred these animals to try to "fix" these attributes and pass them on to future generations of puppies. And this is exactly what led to the unique group that includes the Yorkie's forebears.

The Terrier Factor

To understand your Yorkie, you have to understand terriers. What distinguishes the terriers from other kinds of dogs is their strong drive to dig. The word terrier is derived from the French term, *chien terrier,* meaning "dog of the earth." As a hunting group, terriers specialize in pursuing animals (usually vermin rather than game) that live in dens or burrows. Animals that are cornered in their dens, and/or are defending their young, will fight ferociously. Therefore any dog that would willingly pursue them had to have an uncommon degree of courage. The kind of dog that most admirably filled the twin bills of small size and large heart was the terrier.

In the field, terriers have been used to drive quarry from its burrow for pursuit by hounds, to hold quarry at bay until hunters with guns could arrive or to dig quarry out and engage it themselves. In many cases, terriers were encouraged to hunt independently, living and dying by their own decisions. Anyone obtaining a terrier needs to know that the wonderful feisty temperament they admire comes with its other, less

The modern-day Yorkie has come a long way from the rodent dens of seventeenth and eighteenth century England.

attractive corollary: independence. To this day terriers are considered hardheaded and difficult to train.

The Legacy of Being Small

The group of dogs called terriers was developed in the fourteenth through nineteenth centuries, mostly in the British Isles. Throughout most of its early history, "Merry Old England" had been a two-class society. The upper classes owned the land and all that grew, lived or moved upon it, and the lower, peasant class owned the shirts on their backs, if they were lucky. At that time, an important source of meat for lordly tables was the furred, feathered and tusked wild game of the forest and field. To help bring down this game, noblemen employed huntsmen who in turn used large coursing hounds. The peasants, however, were prohibited from taking game from royal forests; the penalty for "stealing" the king's deer, for instance, was hanging. To help enforce the law, peasants were also prohibited from owning any of the large breeds of dogs suitable for hunting. Small dogs, however, were permitted, and there wasn't likely to be much objection if the dogs hunted the small, unsavory varmints that lived below ground. Thus the stage was set for a historical association between the poor and a small rugged dog with a strong hunting instinct.

Terriers further developed as specialists in different terrain and for different quarry species. In general, the English Terriers were longer legged, with smooth coats

---

WHERE DID DOGS COME FROM?

It can be argued that dogs were right there at man's side from the beginning of time. As soon as human beings began to document their own existence, the dog was among their drawings and inscriptions. Dogs were not just friends, they served a purpose: There were dogs to hunt birds, pull sleds, herd sheep, burrow after rats—even sit in laps! What your dog was originally bred to do influences the way it behaves. The American Kennel Club recognizes over 140 breeds, and there are hundreds more distinct breeds around the world. To make sense of the breeds, they are grouped according to their size or function. The AKC has seven groups:

1) Sporting, 2) Working,
3) Herding, 4) Hounds,
5) Terriers, 6) Toys,
7) Non-sporting

Can you name a breed from each group? Here's some help: (1) Golden Retriever; (2) Doberman Pinscher; (3) Collie; (4) Beagle; (5) Scottish Terrier; (6) Maltese; and (7) Dalmatian. All modern domestic dogs (*Canis familiaris*) are related, however different they look, and are all descended from *Canis lupus*, the gray wolf.

and folded ears, and hunted fox, otter, woodchuck and badger. In contrast, the Scottish Terriers were short-legged, with erect ears and long, harsh coats. They hunted rats, ferrets and weasels as well as rabbits and ground squirrel. It is from the Scottish stock that the Yorkie is descended.

The coat of this Yorkie, Ch. Yankee Kitty, born in 1921, is somewhat more wiry than that of most contemporary Yorkies.

Made in England

As its name implies, the Yorkshire Terrier is a product of Yorkshire County in northern England. This remote and rugged region was made familiar to millions through the best-selling *All Creatures Great and Small* series of books, and consequent long-running television series, by country veterinarian James Herriot. By the middle of the nineteenth century, the engine of England's industrial revolution was running full tilt in Yorkshire. In addition to agriculture and livestock production, the area's rich deposits of coal and iron helped fuel the revolution's new industries, including textiles.

In search of work, weavers and other craftsmen had come to Yorkshire from Scotland, bringing with them several different varieties of small long-coated terriers. These so-called Scottish Terriers found ready work themselves in controlling the rodent populations in Yorkshire's mills, mines and factories. On weekends,

FAMOUS OWNERS OF THE YORKSHIRE TERRIER

Helen Hayes

Audrey Hepburn

Tama Janowitz

Liberace

Barbara Mandrell

Richard Nixon

Gilda Radner

Joan Rivers

the dogs' owners were not above a bit of sport, wagering on whose terrier could dispatch the largest number of rats in a given length of time.

While experts are not agreed on exactly which breeds have made up the Yorkshire Terrier, certain breeds are commonly thought to be its main forebears. The possible source of the dog's size, coat length and blue/black color are the Clydesdale, Paisley, Skye and Waterside Terriers, all Scottish breeds brought to England at various points throughout history. Additionally, the English Black and Tan Terrier seems to be the most likely precursor to have lent the Yorkie breed its signature color pattern.

This head study is the only known painting made during the life of Huddersfield Ben, the breed patriarch.

One bit of Yorkie history we do know for sure is that in 1865, in or around the town of Huddersfield, in Yorkshire County, a dog named Ben was born. In his short life (he died of an accident when only six years old), he won many prizes at dog shows but also in ratting contests. By today's standards, Ben was a large dog, with only a medium-length coat, no doubt partly due to the active life he led. This dog, known as Huddersfield Ben, is universally acknowledged as the father of the Yorkshire Terrier.

18

The Yorkie in America

The Yorkie has been a popular breed in the United States since the turn of the century. Yorkies have been entered in shows in America since 1878; the first Yorkie was registered with the AKC in 1885, making it one of the first twenty-five breeds to be approved for registration by the AKC. Yorkies have been in high demand for the ensuing one hundred ten years as one of the most popular Toy breeds and, for the past decade or so, near the top ten of all breeds.

Ch. Cede Higgens, winner of Best in Show at the 1978 Westminster Kennel Club show.

In 1978 a Yorkie won the coveted Best in Show award at the prestigious Westminster Kennel Club show, the first and only member of its breed ever to do so. The dog to win this prize was Champion Cede Higgens, a male dog owned by Charles and Barbara Switzer of Seattle, Washington.

Yorkies and You and Me

American Yorkies are predominantly house and apartment dogs, often living in multiple-Yorkie households, supporting the idea that if one is good, more are better and many are best! For obvious reasons, Yorkies have great appeal for people with limited space, and because they are small enough to be paper-trained, they are ideal companions for busy people who may get stuck at the office. Still, it's important to remember that your Yorkie is very much a dog who will love to be out and about in the world. Some argue that if Yorkies are never taken out, they don't miss it. But I feel strongly that a Yorkie simply can never be all that

nature intended until she gets the chance to snuffle in a fragrant patch of earth and feel the power of her own ferocious barking upon an errant flock of pigeons in the park. As owners, we need to be very honest about whose best interests we have in mind if we deprive our wee terriers of their instinctual joys.

As previously stated, only Yorkies that are specifically bred, conditioned and trained for the showring will have any chance of competing there. But there are many other kinds of activities where ability, not appearance,

The rapt attention of this Yorkie is typical of the breed's inquisitive nature.

is what counts. For example, any registered Yorkie, including neutered ones, can compete in AKC-licensed obedience, tracking or agility trials, and a dog need not even be registered to participate in other kinds of events (see Chapters 9 and 10 for details). Any kind of training that you give your Yorkie will make her a better companion, you a better owner and your relationship deeper and more gratifying than you ever thought possible.

chapter 3

The **World**
According to the
Yorkshire Terrier

If you've drooled over the dainty Yorkies at dog shows, which lie on satin pillows and look like they wouldn't say boo to a mouse, do not expect your Eliza Doolittle to look or act like that. At heart, the Yorkie is still a scrappy working-class terrier, who has had no say in the matter of becoming a lap dog.

The typical Yorkie personality easily fills the frame of a dog many times its size. If there's one wrong way to go about living with a Yorkie, it is to treat this tiny Toy like a tiny toy!

What Makes a Yorkie Tick?

There's no denying that Yorkies are captivating little imps, filled with energy, high spirits and an inexhaustible enthusiasm for life. Yorkies are also smart and easily trained. If yours doesn't seem to be any of those things, you may be working against, rather than with, the Yorkie's basic nature and temperament. The Wee and I did not get off to a very good start, partly because I was intimidated by her tiny size, but mostly because I just didn't appreciate how much terrier was still in the Yorkshire.

Lest you get the idea that Yorkies are God's perfect creatures, let me hasten to tell you that a Yorkie has the same capacity as the next dog to become spoiled, uncooperative, disagreeable and even aggressive. Obviously a dog so small—and Yorkie puppies are very small—needs to be protected from potential hazards and handled gently (more about this in later chapters). Aside from some health and safety considerations, you'll be far ahead of the game if you pretend your puppy will grow up to weigh twenty pounds. Then every time you're tempted to treat her like an orchid, you'll stop yourself.

YORKIE CHARACTER

Inasmuch as Yorkies are dogs, they have the full range of canine behaviors. They're social creatures who like to know where they fit in the household "pack." They quickly sort out who belongs and who doesn't; they will bark at strangers; they'll be friendly and outgoing or unfriendly and aloof (largely based on how you train them to be); and of course they chew and dig and scratch and groom themselves in

---

A DOG'S SENSES

Sight: With their eyes located farther apart than ours, dogs can detect movement at a greater distance than we can, but they can't see as well up close. They can also see better in less light, but can't distinguish many colors.

Sound: Dogs can hear about four times better than we can, and they can hear high-pitched sounds especially well. Their ancestors, the wolves, howled to let other wolves know where they were; our dogs do the same, but they have a wider range of vocalizations, including barks, whimpers, moans and whines.

Smell: A dog's nose is his greatest sensory organ. His sense of smell is so great he can follow a trail that's weeks old, detect odors diluted to one-millionth the concentration we'd need to notice them, even sniff out a person under water!

Taste: Dogs have fewer taste buds than we do, so they're likelier to try anything—and usually do, which is why it's especially important for their owners to monitor their food intake. Dogs are omnivores, which means they eat meat as well as vegetable matter like grasses and weeds.

Touch: Dogs are social animals and love to be petted, groomed and played with.

front of company. Yorkie owners sometimes forget that their pets speak dog, not English, which means *you* have to learn how to communicate with them, not the other way around.

Communicating with your Yorkie doesn't always require words.

It's also important to realize that every dog is an individual. Some parts of a dog's temperament are inherited from his parents, and while not typical (not what the standard calls for), a few individual Yorkies may be timid or nervous rather than bold. Puppies whose first weeks aren't spent in a loving home with a conscientious breeder may get a bad start in life that will show up as atypical temperament and behavior; these characteristics can sometimes be overcome, but sometimes they can't. Fortunately, the vast majority of Yorkies do seem to be just what the standard calls for: confident, vigorous and self-important. The following are some of the distinctive qualities that are likely to show up in your dog

CHARACTERISTICS OF THE YORKSHIRE TERRIER

Feisty

Independent

Tenacious

Bold

Intelligent

Active

Inquisitive

Barks a lot

TENACITY

Yorkies have astonishing drive and stick-to-it-ive-ness, which are, of course, hunting attributes. Why, then, do we often hear that they're willful and stubborn? In truth, willfulness and perseverance are really the same qualities—the only difference is whether the task at hand is performed at your encouragement or to your dismay. Take a Yorkie into the ordinary, repetitive obedience training class, for example, and you'll see willfulness as art form; give your Yorkie something intrinsically interesting to do, such as chase and retrieve a small floppy object that lends itself to a good shaking, and you'll lose count of the number of times he'll want to play this "game."

Don't think the Yorkie is all surface and no substance; the breed is noted for its intelligence.

Tenacity is most likely to show up when the Yorkie is in his "hunting" mode. Never mind that the prey is a knotted sock or a favorite ball that has rolled out of reach under a table. The Yorkie may well take up a day-long vigil, ignoring repeated calls to dinner and other favorite activities. A bit of milk bone can set the Yorkie off on a three-hour search for the perfect place among the sofa pillows to bury it.

BOLDNESS

Many Yorkie owners tell proud but harrowing tales of the day their Charles or Diana took on the rogue Rottweiler down the street, and it's a rare multi-breed home where the top dog is not the Yorkie. However, bold does not mean aggressive. Bold is what you get when you mix great inquisitiveness, or the instinct to protect, with self-confidence. A recent television program on dogs featured a segment where a single woman's Yorkie sent the woman's date to the emergency room for stitches when it misconstrued the gentleman's friendly smack on the lady's rump. The funny part was that the suffering suitor claimed his assailant was a German Shepherd; admitting to being attacked by a five-pound Yorkshire Terrier would have apparently added insult to injury.

Whether or not you're amused by your Yorkie's boldness, never lose sight of the fact that he can get into trouble. No matter how large his ego, he is still a little dog who can be seriously injured (more about this in later chapters).

INTELLIGENCE

Yorkies are smart as whips. They do well in sports like obedience and agility that require the dog to carry out a complex series of commands, and where success depends on the ability of the dog and handler to communicate with one another. They can learn to recognize an astonishing number of words, distinguish and fetch separate toys in a box by their names and are generally very rewarding for the teacher who likes an apt pupil.

Yorkies also have an uncanny ability to make complex chains of associations—when there's something in it for them. For example, if you get in the habit of taking your Sampson for a ride in the car on Sunday mornings to pick up the paper at the delicatessen across town, where once in a while the shopkeeper gives her a bit of liverwurst, it will not be long before Sam heads for

---

JUST WAIT TILL NEXT TIME!

I'm waiting as patiently as I can. I've been here by the door ever since she made the coffee. I hope they take me behind the apartment building across the street. The trees over there are oak, and oak trees have the most squirrels. Someday I'm going to catch one of those squirrels. *Oooo-wowp!* Oops. Didn't mean to say that out loud. It's just so darn hard to wait.

He's tying his shoes. It won't be long now. Let me look—yep, she's out in the kitchen getting a baggie. *Oooowww* . . . sorry. Open the door already. Let's go, let's go—oooowwwooooo. . . .

I lunge madly as soon as the door opens. The oaks are straight ahead. "Look, Wee, squirrels."

Wowp! Wowp! Where? Where? *Ywp! Ywp!* I can't see them, but I hear them, I smell them, I know they're here. There! Now I see one! Overdrive!

The squirrel is going up the tree. I hear its claws catching in the bark. I try to follow, but it just doesn't work for me. (How do they do that?) I scrabble and scrabble, but I'm still on the ground. Drat! I circle the tree, craning my neck to see the squirrel. Just wait till next time, I tell that squirrel. *Wowp!* And I don't mean maybe.

—The Wee

the front door at the first pealing of a distant church bell. The Wee so loved her walks that we learned never to say the word in vain, and even resorted to spelling it, a solution that worked for a little while before she'd decoded that, too.

The Wee herself is pictured here in this 1981 photograph, wearing a hand-crocheted harness.

ACTIVENESS—IN BODY AND MOUTH

Most tiny dogs are active and quick and the Yorkie is no exception. Someone used to a St. Bernard would likely be inclined to label a Yorkie as hyperactive. In describing the normally active Yorkie, words like darting, dashing, scampering, hopping and bouncing come to mind. A Yorkie who actually walks on his daily walks is quite likely ancient, ill or possibly too hot.

A typical Yorkie loves to keep active, and will most likely insist that you do the same.

Be aware that Yorkies do have a lot to say. It's the terrier in them that prompts the need to bark . . . and bark. On the other hand, when the Yorkie barks, there usually is a reason. Yorkies make excellent watchdogs. They sleep lightly, awaken in a heartbeat and are in motion (and in voice) in the time it takes a larger, more placid dog to lift its head from the floor.

INDEPENDENCE

The final Yorkie characteristic may seem inconsistent with the others, but the well bred, and especially the well handled, Yorkie can be quite content to be near you without necessarily being on your feet at every moment. Yorkies throw themselves into whatever they do, but their small bodies have small fuel tanks, and they know when they need to rest. At these times, the Yorkie is likely to disappear behind the shoes in your closet or into a warm out-of-the-way corner for some downtime. A precursor to this characteristic is also found in the Yorkie's ancestry. Terriers were expected to hunt in the company of handlers or other dogs, but also to have the self-confidence to go out on their own after prey. Owners who are not prepared for their Yorkshire's independence can feel hurt and disappointed. On the other hand, pampered and indulged Yorkies are more likely to be clingy and demanding, while ironically lacking in true terrier self-confidence.

The Yorkie's small size rarely deters him from making his presence know.

More Information on the Yorkshire Terrier

NATIONAL BREED CLUB

Yorkshire Terrier Club of America, Inc. (YTCA)
Ms. Shirley A. Patterson, Secretary
P.O. Box 271
St. Peters, PA 19470-0271
www.ytca.org
The club can send you information on all aspects of
the breed, including the names and addresses of clubs
in your area. Inquire about membership. The YTCA
publishes the quarterly newsletter, *Yorkie Express*, which
is available to club members.

BOOKS

Gewirtz, Elaine Waldorf. *Your Yorkshire Terrier's Life.*
Roseville, California: Prima Publishing, 2000.

Jackson, Janet. *A New Owner's Guide to Yorkshire Terriers.*
Neptune, New Jersey: TFH Publications, 1996.

Kriechenbaumer, Armin. *Yorkshire Terriers: Everything
about Purchase, Care, Nutrition, Breeding Behavior, and
Training.* Hauppauge, New York: Barron's Educational
Series, 1996.

Lemire, Sandra. *Yorkies Head to Tail.* New Orleans,
Louisiana: Paper Chase Press, 1999.

Sameja-Hilliard, Veronica. *The Yorkshire Terrier Today.*
New York: Hungry Minds, Inc., 2000.

MAGAZINES

The Yorkshire Terrier Magazine
9051 Soquel Drive
Aptos, CA 95003
(408) 662-3130

Web Sites

Yorkshire Terrier FAQ
www.k9web.com/dog-faqs/breeds/yorkies.html
This Web page highlights specifics of the breed, including its history, physical characteristics and temperament.

The Yorkshire Terrier Web Ring
www.geocities.com/Heartland/1824/yorkiering.html
Visit this Yorkie-loving site to connect with other breed enthusiasts. Links to chat rooms, information centers and breed rescue organizations are provided.

Yorkshire Terrier National Rescue, Inc. (YTNR)
www.yorkshireterrierrescue.com
The YTNR is dedicated to finding the best possible homes for Yorkshire Terriers in need, regardless of age or any potential handicaps. Its bi-monthly, online newsletter reports on placement success stories and promotes adoptable Yorkies.

Yorkshire Terrier Homepage
www.yorkie.ch/hunde/yorkies/yorklink.htm
Visit this extensive Web site to experience an international love affair with Yorkies. Photographs and information on these terriers is posted from around the globe.

Yorkie Lane
www.yorkielane.com
Stop by Yorkie Lane for everything a Yorkie lover's heart could desire, including recipes for favorite dog treats, grooming tips perfect for use on silky Yorkie coats and information on how to search for a responsible Yorkie breeder. An assortment of Yorkies speak their minds on their individual Web pages, allowing readers enjoyable insight into these plucky terriers.

Mailing List

Yorkie Mailing List
To subscribe, send e-mail to:
LISTSERV@APPLE.EASE.LSOFT.COM. In the body of the message, simply write: SUBSCRIBE YORKIE-L.

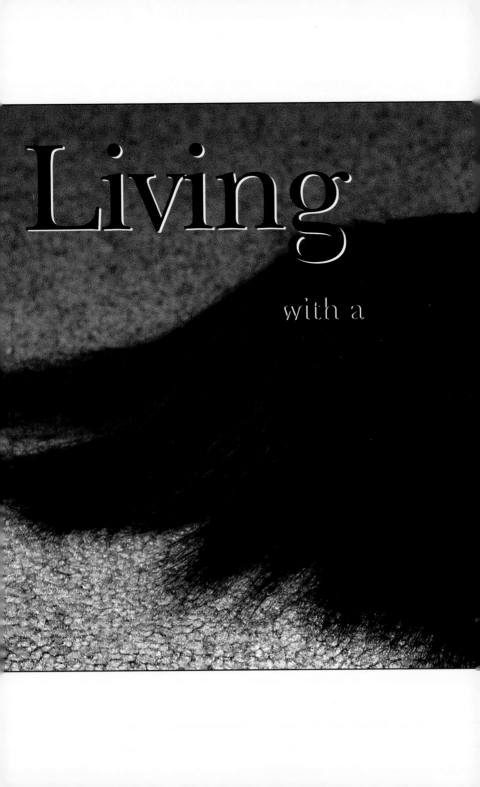

Living

with a

part two

Yorkshire Terrier

chapter 4

Bringing Your
Yorkshire Terrier
Home

You're almost there! Red ink marks the date on the calendar when you get to bring home your brand new puppy. Whether or not it's your first puppy or just your first Yorkie, this is a time of happy anticipation. It should also be a time of busy preparation.

What's to prepare, you ask? Well, would you bring a human baby home without at least a box of diapers and a spit cloth? A puppy requires as much planning, and maybe more. After all, a human baby will stay put for a few months until you figure out what you're doing. To get your puppy off on the right foot, here are some things to line up ahead of time.

Safety Items

You might think the first order of business is food, but unless the Stork Dog drops your puppy down the chimney, you'll have to pick her up somewhere and bring her home. Accidents happen. To be safe, the puppy should wear a harness, or a collar and leash, and an ID tag—even if her feet never touch the ground. You may be tempted to just slip Mighty Mite into your pocket or place her beside you on the car seat, but don't. Invest up front in a secure travel case that Mite will come to associate with good times and hop into eagerly whenever you pick up your keys. There are wonderful lightweight shoulder bags on the market that are designed for cats and small dogs. They're perfect for taking your Yorkie shopping or on the bus; their drawback is that they don't offer the protection of a fiberglass or metal carrier.

Collar   An excellent first collar for a tiny Yorkie puppy is a nylon buckle collar. It is lightweight, inexpensive and comes in a variety of plain and designer colors. Find the correct size by measuring around Mite's neck, then adding two inches. Expect to replace this collar once or twice as Mite grows; adjustable collars which "grow" with puppies' necks are generally too bulky for a neck as tiny as a Yorkie's.

Lead   For Mighty Mite's first lead, also called a leash, choose nylon of about the same width as the collar, equipped with a swivel and safety snap. (If you like the look and feel of leather, wait until the puppy is both a little more substantial and is finished teething— roughly six months of age.) Most leads come in four- or six-foot lengths; the shorter size is plenty long enough for your Yorkie.

Harness   An alternative to the collar and lead is the harness. I like harnesses for Yorkies for two reasons: They can't possibly injure the dog's (and especially the puppy's) delicate neck and throat, as collars can; and harnesses can be used to safely lift the entire dog out of harm's way, should that ever be necessary.

PUPPY ESSENTIALS

Your new puppy will need:

food bowl

water bowl

collar

leash

I.D. tag

bed

crate

toys

grooming supplies

ID Tag   Many a puppy has been tragically lost while her owner was intending to get an identification tag. Avoid this heartbreak by ordering your puppy's tag in advance. If you haven't settled on a name, just use "puppy"; after all, the critical information is your name and telephone numbers (daytime and evening). When you take your puppy to the veterinarian, ask about permanent identification (tattooing or microchip implantation). Tags can become lost or removed; a tattoo, usually on the inner thigh, or a microchip, implanted by a veterinarian at the back of the neck, is permanent. Should your dog ever become lost, a registered tattoo number or a microchip will provide a means of tracing your dog back to you.

Safe Places

MacDuff will be tiny when you bring him home, but don't wait until you walk through the door with him to consider which areas he'll have access to until he's housetrained and the methods you'll use to keep him there. The critical considerations are that he not be isolated from you any more than necessary, but that he be restricted at first to a small area that can be easily cleaned (no rugs or carpeting!). A finished basement play room, a pantry or laundry room off the kitchen are not good ideas. Your puppy needs to be where you are.

While your Yorkie may look irresistibly cute in a bag like this, it's probably safer to bring your puppy home in proper equipment.

Whichever room you choose should be one that can be easily puppy-proofed. A bright kitchen or even part of a kitchen is ideal for the daytime, though you probably will want MacDuff to sleep in your room at night (see "Bed/Crate," below). Use babygates to section off a large room, or to keep Duffy from falling down the cellar stairs. The only drawback to kitchens is that they invariably are full of dangerous cleaning products, ant and roach traps and other hazards. Protect your Yorkie by figuring out ahead of time how to keep all cupboard doors securely fastened, the contents of the garbage pail or cat's litter box inaccessible and MacDuff himself away from the stove where boiling liquids or spattering grease may land on him.

Dishes

The important subject of what to feed your puppy will be covered in detail in Chapter 5. But whatever your choice of food, your puppy will need separate bowls for food and water. Dishes should be non-chewable, impossible to tip over and easy to clean. Beware of hand-painted ceramics or dishes not expressly intended for food, as paints may contain lead or other toxic substances. You can never go wrong with stainless steel or plain glass.

A puppy carrier like this one might be useful on long-distance outings.

Bed/Crate

A dog crate (also called a kennel or cage) is the piece of equipment that is going to assure that your puppy is easily housetrained, and that she has a place of her own for sleeping or retreating to when, like Greta Garbo, she wants to be alone. Some owners use a crate to housetrain their dog, then replace it later with a "real" dog bed. This is a personal choice, but from the dog's point of view, it's not necessary. If you use the crate correctly, your Yorkie will never want or need another bed.

What's that you say? You thought that Hercules would just sleep in your bed? Ah, yes; Hercules would like that. But here's the thing to think about: Dogs have a

35

hard enough time learning all the "rules" of living in a human pack. If the rules keep changing, they are lost. What this means is that you need to think your way past what might seem like a good idea for now, and think instead in terms of lifelong habits. So unless you're going to want Herkie to sleep with you forever—no matter who else shares the bed, or how old, or sick, or possibly smelly the dog may become due to conditions beyond his control or yours—then don't start off that way. A crate set up by your bed will offer all the benefits of having the puppy, and later the dog, close by, but will avoid the pitfalls.

Dog crates come in two basic types: the mostly solid fiberglass or molded plastic type approved by airlines, and the mostly open wire crates. Plastic crates are lightweight and easy to clean. Wire crates permit air to circulate more readily, allow you to observe the puppy and allow the puppy to feel less isolated. Place a cuddly cotton blanket or towel in the crate—no synthetics, treated fabrics or foam.

Dog crates are not inexpensive. Luckily, the smallest size is also the cheapest. The right size will allow your dog, when fully grown, to stand with her head up, to turn around, stretch and sleep comfortably. Bigger than that is not better. If you're thinking of getting two Yorkies, and figure you'll just get a larger crate that they can share, it is not a good idea. Each Yorkie deserves her own bed, her own private place. Best buddies will be happy to be side by side; they don't need to be on top of each other.

HOUSEHOLD DANGERS

Curious puppies and inquisitive dogs get into trouble not because they are bad, but simply because they want to investigate the world around them. It's our job to protect our dogs from harmful substances, like the following:

IN THE HOUSE

cleaners, especially pine oil

perfumes, colognes, aftershaves

medications, vitamins

office and craft supplies

electric cords

chicken or turkey bones

chocolate

some house and garden plants, like ivy, oleander and poinsettia

IN THE GARAGE

antifreeze

garden supplies, like snail and slug bait, pesticides, fertilizers, mouse and rat poisons

Chews and Toys

Something that's safe and satisfying for a puppy to chew on is more a matter of developmental necessity than the word toy suggests. Puppies use their mouths to investigate their environment. In the world of people, however, most of that environment is dangerous or just off-limits to sharp little teeth. It is also your responsibility to remove hazardous objects around the house—in essence, anything at all that can be chewed and/or swallowed.

The open arms of a loving owner often make the best resting place for a worn-out Yorkie.

Some designated "chew toys" are edible (rawhide, pigs' ears, beef hooves) and some are not (cotton, nylon, vinyl, latex, hard or soft rubber, etc.). While you and I know the difference between the two, your puppy may be a little less savvy; inedible objects are eaten by puppies as a matter of course. Use common sense and natural caution in selecting your puppy's toys, avoiding anything with squeakers or other small parts to choke on. To meet Fang's need to chew, the chewies you select should be of small enough gauge to fit into the back of his mouth where the jaw hinges.

Grooming and Medical Supplies

Grooming is a big part of owning a Yorkie, and will be covered in detail in Chapter 6. At this point I just want to say that grooming supplies are something that you should think about and budget for. Purchasing at least a few of the basics should be among the things you plan to do prior to your puppy's arrival. Likewise, there are a number of medical supplies that you should purchase and have on hand before you might need them.

These are given in Chapter 7. For now, just make a note on your "to do" list to set up your grooming and medical supply kits, and to be thinking about a convenient and easy-to-find place in which to store them.

Quality Veterinary Services

Now is also the time to find a veterinarian for your puppy. Resist the temptation to just go to whomever is closest. Ask other dog owners for references, then visit two or three hospitals to check them out. Some factors to consider might be whether the clinic provides after-hours or emergency service, how many veterinarians share the practice and whether they represent different areas of expertise (your Yorkie can benefit, for example, from both traditional and more holistic approaches). As you're talking to the veterinarian and his or her receptionist, notice if you feel comfortable. Yorkies are so popular that it's unlikely a veterinarian won't have some in his or her practice, but ask. You want a doctor who is familiar and comfortable with the special medical issues of the Yorkie.

Your puppy's young coat will require daily attention in just a few short months.

Time and Money

The final items to plan for are time and money. Dogs do take time—always when they're very young, often when they're very old. In the beginning weeks and months, figure that you will be spending at least an hour a day on puppy stuff—handling and grooming, housetraining, teaching basic manners and socializing, preparing food, cleaning up puddles, getting your questions answered, and, of course, cooing and cuddling. Always bring a new puppy home when you can set aside time for getting her settled in. A long weekend is the minimum; a few weeks would be ideal. Keep the first few days as calm as possible—no parade of visitors, no excited children, just you and puppy getting to know each other.

Eventually, Yorkie puppy chores will be replaced by adult maintenance routines, but the time requirement will not change much. By the time the puppy has all of her shots and is on a regular walking/exercise schedule, plan to devote ten or fifteen minutes to that schedule, four times a day. The Wee used to walk a minimum of a mile every day, and this kept her in excellent physical condition; nevertheless, short legs cannot walk a mile as fast as long ones, so it was time that had to be budgeted for. It's true that Yorkies can probably get all the exercise they need running around the house, jumping up and down from the bed or the sofa, but that's a pale substitute for a brisk walk in the wide fragrant world.

As your Yorkie's coat grows, you will need to budget time for grooming; figure an average of ten minutes for this daily task. If you make the mistake of neglecting your daily touch-ups, you will be facing a much larger task on the weekend.

Your Yorkie will be happiest when allowed to experience the fragrant outdoors.

Money is another matter. Dogs typically have high start-up costs, moderate maintenance costs through the bulk of their lives and then high old-age costs. Although it's no more possible to put a price on the joy and pleasure of a dog than on that of a child, many people fail to remember that responsible dog care does cost money. Time spent budgeting for the near and longer term is time very well spent. You might even want to think about putting some money aside every month for your Yorkie, just as you might for a child; that way you'll always be able to afford the quality of care that a precious companion deserves.

chapter 5

Feeding
Your
Yorkshire
Terrier

The first commandment of feeding a new puppy, or even an older dog, is "Thou shalt make no abrupt changes." Sudden switches in the type or quantity of food, or in water, can bring on stomach upsets and diarrhea, particularly in delicate tums like your Yorkie's. So the first thing to do is find out what kind and amount of food the puppy has been eating and obtain about a week's supply. If you do intend to switch to a different food, make the changeover gradually by mixing the new and old foods together during the course of a week. If you pick your puppy up from a breeder, ask for a bottle of the water the puppy is used to, and make a gradual changeover to your water also. (There are many good reasons to obtain your puppy from a conscientious breeder. That person's willingness to help your puppy make a smooth transition into your home is one of them.)

So much for rules. Here are other things to think about in relation to food and feeding.

Choices, Choices

There are almost too many food choices available to today's dog owner. It can make you think that there must be a single best food or combination of foods for your Yorkie, and that it's your job to figure out what it is. Not so. Your Yorkie will probably do well on most commercial diets. Make sure any food you buy is specified for dogs and that it carries the words "complete and balanced" or "nutritionally complete" on the label. A drawback to commercial diets is that they are generally over-processed, and have therefore lost many of the food's original nutrients.

Many Yorkie specialists feed one brand exclusively when it works well for them. That approach has its attractions. However, my feeling is that the Yorkie who is fed many different foods is less likely to become finicky or to suffer digestive upsets if you have to change his diet for some reason. Try to relax about mealtime. Yorkies are good eaters unless they are allowed to become fusspots. Incidentally, if I overdo the advice to relax, it's because I was unable to follow that advice when The Wee was a wee thing. If you've never had a puppy

TYPES OF FOODS/TREATS

There are three types of commercially available dog food—dry, canned and semimoist—and a huge assortment of treats (lucky dogs!) to feed your dog. Which should you choose?

Dry and canned foods contain similar ingredients. The primary difference between them is their moisture content. The moisture is not just water. It's blood and broth, too, the very things that dogs adore. So while canned food is more palatable, dry food is more economical, convenient and effective in controlling tartar buildup. Most owners feed a 25% canned/75% dry diet to give their dogs the benefit of both. Just be sure your dog is getting the nutrition he needs (you and your veterinarian can determine this).

Semimoist foods have the flavor dogs love and the convenience owners want. However, they tend to contain excessive amounts of artificial colors and preservatives.

Dog treats come in every size, shape and flavor imaginable, from organic cookies shaped like postmen to beefy chew sticks. Dogs seem to love them all, so enjoy the variety. Just be sure not to overindulge your dog. Factor treats into her regular meal sizes.

as tiny as a Yorkie, it can be hard to believe they aren't desperately delicate. They aren't, as long as you avoid puppies advertised as "teacups" or "miniatures" (there are no such classifications of Yorkies) and puppies younger than about ten weeks.

Many Yorkies are picky about their food.

Dry or Canned?

This is really a matter of choice. Some Yorkies prefer one, some the other; most will eat both if they're fed both. Dry food helps clean tartar from the teeth, but because it has no moisture, puppies who eat only dry food will drink a lot of water. This can complicate housetraining. For this reason, I recommend feeding canned food until your puppy is housebroken.

Ages and Stages

Most brand-name manufacturers now offer products for the major stages of a dog's life: puppy, adult, senior, high-performance and "lite." Dogs who lived and died before these were available did just fine without them, but why not take advantage? Again, keep a relaxed attitude. If you run out of puppy food, it's not going to hurt to feed something else for a day or two.

Natural and Organic

Organically grown natural foods are becoming more and more popular for people and for pets. Personally, I'm all for them. There's something reassuring about looking at a list of natural ingredients (you should always check ingredients) and seeing things that you can recognize as foods rather than a long list of chemical compounds. Organically grown foods and meats have been produced without pesticides and hormones, which add nothing beneficial to the food and can be harmful.

Ingredients you don't want to see are animal or poultry by-products, as they may include indigestible parts such as fur, feathers, claws, beaks, etc. You also don't want to see additions such as artificial colors or flavorings, sweeteners or sugars. The question of preservatives is less easily answered. Ideally, you could do without them, but this choice requires vigilant attention to shelf life. It also means that you must feel confident that your shopkeeper is careful about the conditions under which products are shipped and kept in the store. The best of all possible situations would be if your Yorkie's food (and your own) could be grown organically in the next town and delivered fresh to your doorstep.

Until that day arrives, however, be assured that, in most cases, your Yorkie can safely eat from the supermarket shelf.

How Much and How Often

There's a fairly simple formula for figuring out how often to feed your puppy, based on his age:

8 weeks to 12 weeks	4x a day	Morning, early afternoon, early evening and before bed
12 weeks to 18 weeks	3x a day	Morning, early evening and before bed
Over 18 weeks	2x a day	Morning, early evening

Once eighteen weeks old, the Yorkie should remain on two meals a day. It is too much work for his digestive system to take in and process enough food at one meal to meet his energy needs for an entire day.

There is also an easy formula for the amount to feed your Yorkie. Figure one tablespoon of food per meal for each pound that the Yorkie weighs. Thus a one-pound puppy needs one tablespoon of food at each meal. If the puppy weighs four pounds, he will need approximately four tablespoons of food per meal—though he will be eating fewer times a day.

Keep in mind that these are rough estimates. Your puppy may need either a little more or a little less. Guidelines are only that; your best guide to how much to feed your Yorkie is your Yorkie. If he leaves food in his dish, he needs that much less. If he cleans his bowl and still seems hungry, offer just a tiny bit more. And once again, try to relax. A puppy this age probably won't overeat, and if one or two meals are a little skimpy, the world won't end.

Supplements and Special Diets

Supplements are intended to compensate for nutritional deficiencies, so you will not need to provide your Yorkie with any supplements unless instructed to do so by your veterinarian. A balanced diet provides all necessary nutrients in correct proportions. Likewise, special diets are intended as therapy. That is, they are prescribed by your veterinarian to help treat various conditions such as allergies or

---

HOW TO READ THE DOG FOOD LABEL

With so many choices on the market, how can you be sure you are feeding the right food for your dog? The information is all there on the label—if you know what you're looking for.

Look for the nutritional claim right up top. Is the food "100% nutritionally complete"? If so, it's for nearly all life stages; "growth and maintenance," on the other hand, is for early development; puppy foods are marked as such, as are foods for senior dogs.

Ingredients are listed in descending order by weight. The first three or four ingredients will tell you the bulk of what the food contains. Look for the highest-quality ingredients, like meats and grains, to be among them.

The Guaranteed Analysis tells you what levels of protein, fat, fiber and moisture are in the food, in that order. While these numbers are meaningful, they won't tell you much about the quality of the food. Nutritional value is in the dry matter, not the moisture content.

In many ways, seeing is believing. If your dog has bright eyes, a shiny coat, a good appetite and a good energy level, chances are his diet's fine. Your dog's breeder and your veterinarian are good sources of advice if you're still confused.

diseases of the kidney, heart or liver. It would be a mistake to feed your Yorkie one of these diets without a veterinarian's instruction to do so.

Snacks and Treats

Once your puppy is doing well on a regular feeding schedule, you can offer occasional snacks if there's some reason to do so. For instance, if you take an especially long walk one day, or if the puppy plays more vigorously than usual or has a particularly exciting morning romping with a friend, these are occasions when a snack makes sense; the puppy probably could use a little energy boost.

Treats, on the other hand, are best reserved as training aides. A food lure or treat is an effective way to induce a puppy or dog to learn new behaviors or to reinforce behavior you want the puppy to retain. Very small pieces of cheese or some other nutritious food with a strong aroma make perfect training treats. Offering treats at random times and for no apparent reason diminishes their effectiveness as training tools.

Keep in mind that both snacks and treats are still food. The caloric content of any snacks and treats offered during the day must be calculated and subtracted from the day's overall ration. If you neglect to do this for long, you will find your Yorkie is starting to get thick. Excess weight in dogs creates the same problems as it does in people!

HOW MANY MEALS A DAY?

Individual dogs vary in how much they should eat to maintain a desired body weight—not too fat, but not too thin. Puppies need several meals a day, while older dogs may need only one. Determine how much food keeps your adult dog looking and feeling her best. Then decide how many meals you want to feed with that amount. Like us, most dogs love to eat, and offering two meals a day is more enjoyable for them. If you're worried about overfeeding, make sure you measure correctly and abstain from adding tidbits to the meals.

Whether you feed one or two meals, only leave your dog's food out for the amount of time it takes her to eat it—ten minutes, for example. Freefeeding (when food is available any time) and leisurely meals encourage picky eating. Don't worry if your dog doesn't finish all her dinner in the allotted time. She'll learn she should.

Yorkies Are What They Eat

Along with love and consistency and exercise, providing good food is one of the important things that you do for your Yorkie every day. The neat thing about nutrition is that food and feeding has its visible outcomes: You aren't going to over-, under- or misfeed your Yorkie for long without seeing the telltale signs. You can be reasonably sure that you're hitting the nutritional mark as long as your Yorkie has clear skin and eyes; sports a shiny coat with ribs you can feel beneath it; maintains high spirits and good weight and has well-formed stools that pick up easily.

Feeding Do's and Don'ts

Following a few simple feeding guidelines will help you see that your Yorkie stays in good health and physical condition. Once the dog has settled into your home and feels comfortable, experiment with different foods to see what your Yorkie likes. Keep in mind that this experimentation should not be overly abrupt. While you do this, keep a food diary so that you can monitor the results of offering different foods and varying

Snacks and treats are best reserved for training and behavior reinforcement.

amounts. Pick a quiet, out-of-the-way spot for your Yorkie to eat and be sure to schedule the feedings for the same times every day. Doing this will help to establish good eating and elimination habits. Keeping to a schedule like this means that you have to keep your own eating schedule fairly regular as well; it's definitely a good idea to feed your Yorkie after you eat—dogs understand that leaders eat first. As for snacks, if you do decide to give them to your Yorkie periodically, try to make them nutritious. Whole foods like bits of raw carrots, green beans, apples or bananas are good examples.

When it comes to feeding your Yorkie, there are just as many things that you shouldn't do as there are things that you should. Again, don't switch food or water abruptly, and don't leave food down for any longer than ten or fifteen minutes. If the dog clearly has an aversion to a particular flavor or brand of food, don't buy it again. You should also discontinue feeding your Yorkie a particular food if you find that it gives him gas, or causes a loose or hard, dry stool. Don't feed him generic foods; raw or undercooked pork, fish or seafood; and definitely avoid milk, onions (raw or cooked) and especially chocolate.

chapter 6

Grooming
Your
Yorkshire
Terrier

It's wonderful that life offers so many options, but sometimes it's easier when there's only one right answer. That's the way it is with grooming the Yorkshire Terrier: It has to be done. It doesn't matter whether your Yorkie's coat is stupendous, superb, satisfactory or only so-so—she still has to be groomed. This, however, really is good news. Grooming Rapunzel is one of the best ways there is to get to know her intimately, and it will become a soothing ritual for you both—provided you get off on the right foot.

Beginning at the Beginning

If you acquired Rapunzel from a conscientious breeder, undoubtedly she's already been introduced to the basics of being groomed: a little light brushing, having her nails clipped, a bit of scissoring around her ears and feet, maybe even her first bath. Whatever the breeder did or didn't do, the most important aspect was gently initiating the puppy at a very early age to procedures that will become as much a part of her life as eating.

So if Rapunzel has had this exposure, you're ahead of the game. If she hasn't, the time for you to start is now. It doesn't matter that her coat is only an inch long. It's her attitude you're "grooming" at this point. Her acceptance, your skills and confidence and her coat will all grow together.

What You'll Need

You don't need a lot of fancy supplies to care for your Yorkie—in the beginning or ever. Down the road, if you find yourself really "getting into" the grooming thing, you may want to invest in additional supplies. For now, the items in the grooming tools sidebar, plus the following additional items should suffice: a sponge, cotton balls, a non-slip mat for the tub, a spray attachment for the faucet, a hair dryer, and a baby hair clasp or small rubber bands.

Setting Up

Just as with feeding, walking, training and everything else, you will want to establish a routine for grooming that your puppy can learn to depend on. The sequence I recommend is as follows: brush, comb, trim, bathe, cut nails, blow dry.

But first, where will you do the grooming? Some people train their Yorkies to lay in their laps or on a table for grooming, turning the body from side to side as necessary. Others groom with the dog standing on a stool, table or countertop. I find there's less strain on my back if I can sit or stand and have the dog at waist height. The obvious and very real danger in this is that you cannot take your eyes or hands off the puppy for one single second. Don't even think about whether Rapunzel will jump—she will!

GROOMING TOOLS

pin brush

slicker brush

flea comb

towel

mat rake

grooming glove

scissors

nail clippers

tooth-cleaning equipment

shampoo

conditioner

clippers

Once you've picked a spot, gather together all your supplies so you can proceed in an orderly way. I wouldn't attempt a full-scale grooming session for several weeks. It will pay off in the long run if you start slowly, spend just a few seconds on each maneuver and concentrate on following the same sequence each time. For instance, first you might run the

brush gently over the puppy's legs, body and head, all in ten seconds, then go over the same areas, in the same order, with the comb, in another ten seconds. As you work, talk softly and calmly to the puppy. You don't want to

A well-groomed Yorkie is a pleasing sight.

wheedle or plead with her to stand still (out of the question anyway!), nor do you want to get gruff or impatient. If you explain to her what you're doing and why, regardless of the fact that she won't understand a single word, you will have automatically adopted the right no-nonsense tone.

Tip: Don't give Rapunzel a chewie or toy to distract her while you groom. She really does have to learn that this is a serious time. Praise her calmly for every few seconds that she is calm and cooperative. And don't ever let her convince you to put down the comb, brush or clippers when she says so; that only teaches her that if she squirms and struggles, you'll stop.

Brushing and Combing

If you grew up in the 1950s, as I did, you brushed your hair one hundred strokes a day because your mother said doing so made it shiny and was good for your scalp. Then you combed your hair to get out the snarls, to put in a part or maybe to draw it all up into a glossy ponytail. Obviously, hair-care strategies for humans have changed dramatically since then. But when it comes to your Yorkie, it's back to the 50s.

Brush first. This separates the hair, distributes oils and feels good. Then, with short downward strokes, comb slowly and carefully. Begin near the tips of the hair and work your way toward the dog's body, feeling for tangles or small matted areas. If you encounter resis-

tance, stop. The smallest tug against a tangle will elicit a piercing yip from your Yorkie that neither of you will soon forget. You don't need it.

Grasp the problem area with your fingers, lifting the coat to make sure you release any tension against

the dog's skin. Then break up the mats with your fingers, the brush or the tip of the comb. Only when you can comb cleanly through the area that was snarled or matted should you release your grip on the coat and comb from the skin outward.

Combing the Yorkie's coat will help get out any tangles.

When you're through combing Rapunzel, the comb should run through smoothly, from the skin to the tips of the hair. Not just down the center of her back, but everywhere: in the armpits, on the insides of the rear legs, behind the ears, on the tops of the feet, at the corners of the mouth. If Rapunzel is a puppy whose coat is just beginning to grow, you shouldn't encounter anything too serious, although eating and drinking can gum up the hair around the mouth, as can stepping in urine puddles mat the hair on the rear feet. During your first grooming sessions, only tackle one small tangle at a time, then move on.

Trimming

There's not much trimming to be done on a Yorkie, and until the hair gets a little longer, you may be snipping air. Still, it's important for both of you to get used to the feel and sound of the scissors. Later on, you may

51

decide you like the look of a "puppy trim," which just means keeping the body coat short and cutting in bangs on the forehead.

Feet   Stand the Yorkie on a table and trim all the way around each foot. When she lifts the foot you're working on (and she will, because dogs are sensitive around their feet), lift the opposite one instead and hold it up—this will force her to stand on the one you're trimming. Lift each foot, place the scissors flat against the pad, and snip any hair that extends beyond the pad (be careful not to pinch the pad with the scissors). Again, end this step when she's standing quietly, not when she's resisting.

A regular groom-ing routine is the only way to keep an active dog looking good, and to save your-self time in the long run.

Ears   Trim away the hair that grows beyond the edges of the top half of the ear. Don't worry about getting right up to the edge until you're more com-fortable. Your Yorkie will be wiggling and tossing her head, but don't try to forcibly restrain her. Concentrate on holding the ear gently but firmly, talking calmly, and going through the motions until she figures out this isn't going to hurt.

Anal/genital region   Your Yorkie will stay cleaner longer if you get in the habit of cutting away the hair that grows around the rectum and genital areas. Practice the motions before you actually cut any hair. Scissoring the genital area is easiest with the dog lying on her back in your lap. Rest one hand on the puppy to steady her—Yorkies are famous for sudden moves.

Bathing

Bathe your Yorkie in a warm room, away from drafts. Puppy's first baths will be stressful, so pick a day when nothing else is going on and when the puppy is feeling and eating well. After her bath, your puppy will probably need to urinate, and then want to be left alone for a nice long rest.

Place the non-slip mat in the sink, then cut a hole over the drain so the water can run out. Attach the hose to the faucet and experiment until the temperature is warm and the flow is light to moderate. Put small plugs of cotton in each of your Yorkie's ears, then stand her on the mat in the sink and reassure her for a minute.

Thoroughly wet the coat and the underside of the dog. Use the sponge to wet her head and face. Shampoo the body, add a bit more water, and use your fingers to work up a lather (don't rub the coat in circles). Wash down each leg and under the feet. Wash the head last by applying the shampoo to the sponge. Try to avoid getting shampoo in the eyes or mouth. Then rinse the whole dog thoroughly, first the head, then the body and legs, then underneath. Make sure every speck of shampoo is out of the coat and off the skin.

Place the puppy on one towel and dry her gently with the other, squeezing as much water as possible into the towel. At this point The Wee always wanted to get down on the floor and tear around for a minute or two, growling and barking and wiping her whole body on the bedspread and slipcovers. Then I would scoop her up again and dry her with the hair dryer (not too hot and not too close to the skin), brushing her coat as it dried.

Show dogs often have their long coats wrapped up in wax paper to keep the ends from getting soiled and broken.

Clipping Nails

Nails can be clipped when they're dry, but dogs seem to mind it less when they're soft from the bath. Unless your Yorkie is angelic, begin by just doing one or two at a time, and take off only the tiny bit that curves down at the tip (viewed from the underside). Yorkies' nails are black and you won't be able to see the vein or "quick" inside; this vein does not extend past the curved portion of the nail, but it will bleed if you nick

Care must be taken not to nick the quick when clipping a Yorkie's nails.

it. It will hurt, and your Yorkie will never forget it. As with other grooming procedures, praise the dog for cooperative behavior and don't let her think that if she resists, you'll desist.

Tip: Lots of walking outdoors on sidewalks can go a long way to keeping your Yorkie's nails short, but you still need to be able to clip them.

Finishing Touches

According to the standard, Yorkies' coats are parted on the face, and from the back of the skull to the end of the tail. Later, you may decide you don't want to be bothered with this, but until then, why not give it a whirl? If your puppy has enough hair for a topknot, comb it up and fasten it in a rubber band or in a clasp. Make sure the hair isn't pulled tight and that you don't accidentally catch any skin in the rubber band. Small ribbons or bits of yarn can be added if you like.

How Often?

A stitch in time saves nine, and keeping your Yorkie's coat clean and mat-free is much easier than trying to correct a neglected coat a month later. Here's the schedule I recommend:

- Brushing and combing—every day
- Cleaning the beard and under the eyes—every day
- Clipping nails—once a week
- Bathing—once a month or as needed

54

chapter 7

Keeping Your
Yorkshire Terrier
Healthy

If "A stitch in time saves nine" is the key to keeping your Yorkie well-groomed, the key to keeping him healthy is "An ounce of prevention is worth a pound of cure." This approach to veterinary care parallels current trends in human medicine, and makes perfect sense in both. With so much emphasis on wellness and well-being, it's an exciting time to be getting a new puppy.

The topics of concern will be covered in the following order and are listed with page numbers for ease of reference:

Genetic Defects

First, the bad news: All pure breeds of dogs are predisposed to some genetic defects and diseases. Some (but not all) defects can be tested for in advance, and conscientious breeders will not breed dogs who carry defective genes that can be passed on to their puppies. The following are the most common defects that afflict Yorkies (among other breeds); be sure to ask your dog's breeder if any of these abnormalities have shown up in his or her dogs. They are listed in alphabetical order.

Collapsing trachea   The walls of the trachea, or windpipe, of many tiny breeds are flaccid and become more so as the dog ages. The first sign of this condition often is an occasional honking cough, especially on exertion (see "Coughing," p. 78), which may become almost constant in later life. Breathing against the obstruction for many years can result in chronic lung disease and other complications. Sometimes the defect can be repaired with surgery and the coughing controlled with cough suppressants. Overweight Yorkies with this defect are likely to suffer more than those who are lean.

Dental Problems   Although some breeders believe that large, strong, tartar-resistant teeth are inherited, the more relevant genetic factor in dental health may be the alignment of the top and bottom jaws and proper placement of teeth in the jaws. Teeth that are crowded together and overlap one another allow food-particles and bacteria to collect, eventually causing gum inflammation, loose teeth and infected roots. Yorkies with crowded teeth should have some of them removed by a veterinarian. Natural healers advocate the use of herbs, fresh whole foods and plenty of hard items to chew in order to promote strong teeth and gums (see "Teeth," p. 67).

Legg-Perthes Disease   As a result of this disease, the head of the femur (thigh bone) degenerates over time. The condition, which appears to result from insufficient circulation to the area, usually afflicts Yorkies when they are young. The symptom is pain in one or both hips, and lameness. The usual remedy is surgery to remove the affected portion of bone. A less drastic approach to try is acupuncture, which may help improve this condition by increasing the supply of blood to the region.

Luxating Patellas   "Slipping kneecaps" on the rear legs, caused by weak ligaments and tendons, are another common defect in Toy breeds (see "Dislocations," p. 86). A Yorkie may have this problem, which the veterinarian can diagnose by physical exam, but be troubled by it only rarely; or the Yorkie may have pain and lameness. If necessary, surgery can improve or completely correct the condition.

Portosystemic Shunt   This is a congenital malformation of the portal vein, the job of which is to bring blood to the liver for cleansing. The presence of a shunt means that the vein either partially or completely bypasses the liver, and the "dirty" blood goes on to poison the heart, brain, lungs and other organs. Symptoms vary widely and can include poor appetite, occasional vomiting and diarrhea, poor coordination, decreased ability to learn, seizures (especially after eating), blindness, coma and death. Diagnosing portosystemic shunt is difficult but necessary, as the only cure is surgery. Not all shunts can be repaired, but early treatment offers the best hope of success.

Progressive Retinal Atrophy (PRA)   PRA is a gradual degeneration of the retina in the eye leading to blindness. Onset of the condition in Yorkies usually is not until five to seven years of age. The first sign is night blindness or hesitancy to move about normally in a darkened room. At this time, conventional medicine offers no cure, nor is there a test that can predict which puppies will develop the disease. There is anecdotal evidence that homeopathic remedies have been effective in slowing and even reversing the degenerative process in some cases.

Partners in Prevention

A KNOWLEDGEABLE, CARING BREEDER

The first thing you can do to prevent illness in your puppy is to buy from a conscientious breeder who has done everything humanly possible to breed healthy puppies. This includes selecting healthy parents, giving good prenatal care to the mother dog, and then making sure the puppies get everything they need in the weeks before they go to their new homes.

Your puppy's breeder will tell you which vaccinations the puppy has already been given and let you know when the next ones are due. Enter this information in a record book designed for keeping track of your dog's health care. Ask her if the puppy has been treated for worms and when follow-up medication is needed. Listen greedily to any health and husbandry tips she has to share about Yorkies in general, her puppies in particular and, most specifically, your own Lamb Chop.

A GOOD VET

My definition of a good vet is someone who emphasizes maintaining health at least as much as curing illness, who doesn't necessarily see a powerful new drug as the first course of action for every problem and who listens to what I have to say about my dog.

I also like a vet who knows Yorkies. In Chapter 4 you were encouraged to shop around for a vet you felt good about, and you were urged to find out if he or she had experience with Yorkshire Terriers. All pure breeds of dogs have their own "stuff" that may be a bit different from what's true for dogs in general. It may be some genetic predispositions that the vet should know about, or the breed's response to anesthesia, or even what kind of temperamental and behavioral characteristics a dog will typically exhibit. From the point of size alone, it stands to reason that a tiny dog like a Yorkie presents different challenges than a Great Dane. If your vet has a Yorkie breeder in his practice, his greater familiarity with Yorkies will be very much to your advantage.

YOU, THE OWNER

Your sense of responsibility for your Yorkie's well-being will go a long way toward assuring that he gets to live a healthy life. Making sure your Yorkie gets regular preventive care from a veterinarian is part of it, but providing a healthy diet, daily exercise and regular grooming are just as important. Beyond that, it's up to you to know what's normal for your Yorkie, and therefore what isn't, when to seek professional help and what to do in an emergency. Making it a daily practice to run your hands over your Yorkie's entire body, feeling for anything out of the ordinary, will prove to be one of the best ways of finding anything amiss with your dog. Think of this daily check as a sort of "massage" for your dog.

A conscientious breeder's first priority will be breeding healthy puppies.

Finally, and with any luck this day is well over a dozen years away, it will be up to you to realize that your Yorkie is getting old and infirm, and that he needs you to take special care of him again. And beyond that, if pain and suffering have no reasonable hope of improvement, it may someday be your duty and responsibility to make the difficult decision to end your dear one's life.

Preventive Veterinary Care

A day or so after you get your new puppy is a good time to visit the veterinarian for Lord Nelson's first exam. Take along a stool specimen to be tested for worm eggs. Also take along Nelson's record book and get in the habit of entering information on the spot. Ask questions. For example, if the vet takes Nelson's temperature, ask him what it is and write it down. If he notes a little clicking in the right rear knee, write that down, too. It's all well and good for this data to be in the clinic files, but it's nice to have an independent file on your dog. Busy vets will not review your dog's entire file each time you go back, but you can, and you can ask the vet to recheck anything that you're concerned about.

Nelson is bound to respond more positively to his new doctor if no vaccinations are given on this visit. Many veterinarians keep tasty treats on hand to help their patients feel less fearful in the future; in case yours doesn't, take something along in your pocket and ask the veterinarian to give it to your puppy.

> **YOUR PUPPY'S VACCINES**
>
> Vaccines are given to prevent your dog from getting an infectious disease like canine distemper or rabies. Vaccines are the ultimate preventive medicine: They're given before your dog ever gets the disease so as to protect him from the disease. That's why it is necessary for your dog to be vaccinated routinely. Puppy vaccines start at eight weeks of age for the five-in-one DHLPP vaccine and are given every three to four weeks until the puppy is sixteen months old. Your veterinarian will put your puppy on a proper schedule and will remind you when to bring in your dog for shots.

PUPPY PREVENTIVE CARE

Review with your veterinarian the types of vaccines your puppy has had, as this will determine when the next series is due. Some Yorkie breeders prefer not to give permanent vaccines to Yorkie puppies before the age of three months. Others feel vaccines should be given for one disease at a time rather than in an all-in-one shot, which they fear may overwhelm the puppy's immune system. The three-year rabies vaccine is considered too painful for Yorkshire Terriers, so ask instead for the one-year vaccine. In fact, The Wee invariably responded to all her vaccinations by getting very hang-dog, refusing to eat and disappearing into the back of the closet for most of a day. Remember that until Lord Nelson is fully immunized, you must keep him away from other dogs, who may be carrying contagious diseases, and from areas where other dogs have been walked.

*Regular visits
to the vet will
help ensure
your Yorkie's
continued
good health.*

Note: There is increasing controversy about vaccines as they are routinely used; there are now alternatives that homeopathic veterinarians claim are more effective and have fewer side effects than the traditional treatments. If this subject interests you, you should look for a veterinarian who uses holistic or homeopathic alternatives in his or her practice.

Other subjects to discuss with your veterinarian at your first visit are any local veterinary issues you should be aware of, such as whether you need to be concerned about heartworms or Lyme disease. Ask the vet to demonstrate anything you're unsure about, such as how much nail to clip off, how to take the puppy's temperature or how to open its mouth for inspection. If the veterinarian does not provide emergency care, find out which emergency clinic he or she uses. Enter this information in the record book, too.

ADULT PREVENTIVE CARE

After your puppy is fully immunized, you may not see the veterinarian again for a year. In all likelihood, you will receive reminders when Lord Nelson is due for follow-up visits. Normally this is on an annual basis, but depending on where you live and what your dog is exposed to, a different schedule may be recommended. The following are the usual items on the "regular" maintenance checklist.

Physical exam The vet will check eyes, ears, mouth, heart and lungs, skin and coat, and palpate internal organs. My vet's office is too small for the doctor to be able to watch even a Yorkie walk back and forth, but ideally that should be a part of your dog's physical exam. Bring any changes you've noticed to the vet's attention. If Lord Nelson has always jumped up on the sofa to harass birds outside the window, but doesn't seem to bother with them anymore, bring this up. Changes in behavior are the best clues we have that something may be bothering our small friends.

Vaccination boosters Again, there is disagreement about whether annual boosters are needed. All vaccines, even rabies, which is the only one required by law, can be waived for a dog that isn't in good health.

Stool samples There are a number of different kinds of worms that your dog can pick up, mostly by ingesting eggs when eating things such as uncooked meat or fish, contaminated soil, infested animal droppings, fleas, etc. Routine worming is not recommended. Even a positive finding in the stool does not always mean a dog needs to be treated if it does not appear ill in any way.

ADVANTAGES OF SPAY/NEUTER

The greatest advantage of spaying (for females) or neutering (for males) your dog is that you are guaranteed your dog will not produce puppies. There are too many puppies already available for too few homes. There are other advantages as well.

ADVANTAGES OF SPAYING

No messy heats.

No "suitors" howling at your windows or waiting in your yard.

Decreased incidences of pyometra (disease of the uterus) and breast cancer.

ADVANTAGES OF NEUTERING

Lessens male aggressive and territorial behaviors, but doesn't affect the dog's personality. Behaviors are often owner-induced, so neutering is not the only answer, but it is a good start.

Prevents the need to roam in search of bitches in season.

Decreased incidences of urogenital diseases.

Heartworm prevention Anywhere there are mosquitoes, your dog is at risk for getting heartworms. This risk is serious; heartworms are potentially fatal. The procedure is to first have the puppy's blood tested to make sure he is not already infested; assuming he is not, you then will give him (usually) one tablet a month. Many veterinarians are now recommending that dogs stay on heartworm preventative all year long. (Personally, I've lived long enough to be skeptical of any drug that's presumed perfectly safe and innocuous for anyone to take forever.) If you choose not to do this, you will need to have your dog's blood rechecked each year before mosquito season begins.

SPECIAL PREVENTIVE CARE: SPAY/NEUTER

Spaying your female Yorkie or neutering your male is heavy-duty prevention. In addition to absolutely preventing innocent puppies from being born with possible genetic diseases you'd have no way of anticipating, consider what else you can absolutely prevent or at least improve the odds against:

- Diseases of the reproductive organs in males and females.
- Mammary tumors in females.
- Complications of pregnancy and giving birth, including death of mother and loss of puppies.
- Messy, stressful heat seasons for females, which are equally stressful for all other unspayed/unneutered dogs in the neighborhood and for their owners, as well.
- Hormone-linked behaviors such as urine marking (in the house!) and aggressiveness.
- Persistent howling and barking by unneutered males when a neighboring female is in season.
- Death-defying attempts to escape from your home and yard to follow the call of nature.
- The addition of even one more unwanted, and eventually destroyed, dog to the thousands that

already populate this country's animal shelters and pounds.

The maximum benefits of spaying are available if done at around eight months, just before a female's first season. Technically speaking, spaying is the removal of the uterus and ovaries. While the surgery is necessary, and relatively simple (it takes only fifteen to twenty minutes), there is reason to be cautious when you decide to have the procedure done to your Yorkie. Too much anesthesia in such a small dog can be particularly dangerous. If your veterinarian has not successfully administered anesthetic to many Yorkshire Terriers, you should insist that he or she consult with a veterinarian who has done so before allowing your vet to operate on your dog. Neutering a male is a relatively minor procedure that involves the removal of the testicles, and generally requires less recovery time than the spay surgery. In either case, follow to the letter all instructions regarding the withholding of food and water prior to surgery.

GERIATRIC PREVENTIVE CARE

Most dogs are considered seniors after they turn seven; for Yorkies, however, this may turn out to be only early middle age. My veterinarian offers a "geriatric preventive exam" for dogs over seven. This includes a urinalysis and complete blood count to screen for various factors and pick up problems that might be developing. Depending on the results, further specific tests for heart, lungs, liver or kidneys might be ordered. The geriatric preventive exam gives the veterinarian a baseline against which to compare future tests.

Knowing Your Yorkie

As the owner of a treasured Yorkie, you can and should feel like a full partner with your veterinarian in maintaining your Yorkie's health and well-being. One way to do this is by making it a point to know what's normal for your dog, so that you'll immediately know when something is off. Even if the information does nothing more than generate a phone call to your veterinarian, often that's enough. In addition to your daily "massage," here are some things you can do:

KNOW YOUR YORKIE'S VITAL SIGNS

Temperature   The normal average temperature for dogs is 101.3 degrees Fahrenheit, although your own dog's normal temperature may be as low as 100 or as high as 102.5. Don't rely on the temperature (or other vital readings) from the veterinarian's office, as the upset of being there can cause changes. Take your dog's temperature at home from time to time, when all is normal, and record it in the record book. By practicing this skill occasionally, your confidence will grow. Whenever you suspect your Yorkie's not well, the first thing to do is find out if he has a fever. Being able to relay this information to your veterinarian or an emergency clinic will help them assess the situation.

To take your Yorkie's temperature, use an infant's rectal thermometer (make sure it's calibrated to the Fahrenheit scale). Shake it down until it registers 96 degrees, then lubricate the bulb with a small amount of petroleum jelly. Lift and firmly hold the dog's tail so he can't sit down, and gently insert the bulb end about one inch into the rectum using a slow, steady, twisting motion. Hold the thermometer in place for three minutes, remove it and wipe it with a tissue, then "read" the height of the (silver) mercury column.

Pulse   A normal resting pulse for dogs is between seventy and one hundred thirty beats per minute. Toy dogs tend to have faster pulses, but certain well-conditioned, athletic dogs in this group do have slower ones.

To take your Yorkie's pulse, have the dog stand while you run your fingers along the inside of one of the back thighs, and stop where the leg attaches to the body. Press firmly with your fingers to feel the pulsation and count the number of beats in a minute (use a watch with a second hand). You can also try to take the pulse over the heart on the left side of the chest, but with all that panting and snuffling in your face, it will probably be harder to do.

Respiration A normal respiration rate is ten to thirty breaths a minute, at rest. Just watch the rise and fall of your Yorkie's chest when he's lying quietly but not in a deep sleep.

Appetite Notice your dog's normal appetite: how much he eats and how fast, as well as what affects his appetite (excitement, thunderstorms, company, being in a strange place). There's no right or wrong; what's important is what's normal for your dog.

This finger glove, which has bristles on one side, is a handy tool for cleaning Yorkie teeth.

Bowel movements and urine Make a point of noticing your dog's regular bowel and urinary habits. What's the frequency? The quantity, consistency, color? Any change in either is a sign to be looked into.

Behavior Changes in your Yorkie's behavior (when Sweetie Pie suddenly snaps or Joe Kool starts gnawing his feet) or attitude (when Fearless Franny cowers behind your skirts or Iron Mike lets the tug toy fall from his mouth) can be more significant than physiological changes. The thing to remember is this: Dogs don't suddenly change their habits or their minds. The cause may be physical, emotional or environmental, but you can't know which until you investigate. Always bring changes in behavior to the attention of your veterinarian.

Home Check-ups

Routinely checking out your Yorkie's physical condition is no big deal. It happens naturally during the grooming process—all the more reason for treasuring that time together. All abnormal findings mean a prompt visit to the veterinarian, as these conditions can become much more difficult to treat if neglected.

In most cases you will be given medications and other treatments to administer at home.

Eyes Some secretions are normal. Problems can be prevented by a few simple practices: keep hair out of the eyes; clean accumulated brownish matter from the corners of your Yorkie's eyes daily; don't cut hair beneath the eyes, as short ends may then stick into the eyes; and don't let your Yorkie ride with his head outside the car.

Watch for these signs of abnormality in the eyes: thick, stringy discharge; yellow or white discharge; excessive tearing; excessive dryness; redness; squinting.

Ears Yorkie ears are pinkish inside, with a dry and slightly waxy feel. A few wisps of hair may be visible in the canal. Prevent problems by keeping ears dry; clean only with cotton swabs moistened with mineral oil.

Watch for these signs of abnormality in the ears: discharge or any accumulated debris; large amounts or a wad of hair inside the ear; redness; swollen appearance; odor; areas warm and sensitive to the touch.

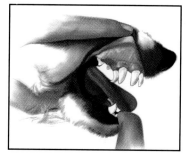

Teeth The Yorkie's top and bottom teeth should meet and be clean and each tooth should have its own space in the jaw. Prevent problems by starting during puppyhood to clean your Yorkie's teeth with a bit of gauze or a thin washcloth wrapped around your finger. Dip the cloth in a paste of baking soda and water.

Check your dog's teeth frequently and brush them regularly.

Watch for these signs of abnormality in the teeth: teeth crowded together and overlapping; double teeth (usually the canines); tan or brown matter on teeth; bad odor; swollen, red gums.

Skin and Coat The skin should be clean and supple, the brushed coat should be lustrous. Yorkie coats come in three varieties: silky, cottony and woolly. The silky coat feels cool and has a metallic sheen; cottony and woolly coats have a warm feel and even though they cannot gleam like a silky coat, they still can have a healthy luster. To prevent problems, make sure your Yorkie has a good diet, lots of exercise, no worms or other parasites and lives in a happy, loving home. Also, keep the heat in your home at a moderate level, and use a humidifier to add moisture to the air.

IDENTIFYING YOUR DOG

It's a terrible thing to think about, but your dog could somehow, someday, get lost or stolen. How would you get him back? Your best bet would be to have some form of identification on your dog. You can choose from a collar and tags, a tattoo, a microchip or a combination of these three.

Every dog should wear a buckle collar with identification tags. They are the quickest and easiest way for a stranger to identify your dog. It's best to inscribe the tags with your name and phone number; you don't need to include your dog's name.

There are two ways to permanently identify your dog. The first is a tattoo, placed on the inside of your dog's thigh. The tattoo should be your social security number or your dog's AKC registration number.

The second is a microchip, a rice-sized pellet that's inserted under the dog's skin at the base of the neck, between the shoulder blades. When a scanner is passed over the dog, it will beep, notifying the person that the dog has a chip. The scanner will then show a code, identifying the dog. Microchips are becoming more and more popular and are certainly the wave of the future.

Watch for these signs of abnormality in the skin and coat: brittle, broken hair; thinning or bare patches; dry or oily scales; a dull, lifeless coat; bad odor; cysts; scabs or other growths on the skin.

Anal/Genital Region   The anal/genital region of your Yorkie, especially if the dog has been spayed or neutered, should not preoccupy the dog, except for proper cleaning after urinating. To prevent problems, spay or neuter your dog and have your veterinarian promptly investigate any excessive licking or fussing with this area.

If the anal sacs (two small glands near the anus) have become clogged with glandular secretions normally released during bowel movements, the contents will have to be squeezed out. If more fiber in the diet and increased exercise don't prevent the problem from recurring, your veterinarian may instruct you in emptying the glands yourself.

Watch for these signs of abnormality in the anal/genital region: inflammation or discharge from penis or vagina; odor; swollen or reddened area around anus; "scooting" (when a dog drags his rear along the ground).

Overall Appearance Your Yorkie should be a lean, firm, muscular package. (You wish you had a body like that!) His limbs should be straight, his back level, his head held high and his tail should wag a lot. To prevent problems in overall conditioning, make sure your Yorkie is allowed to live the active, vigorous life of a dog, not a toy.

Watch for these signs of abnormality in overall appearance: poor muscle tone; too little or too much weight; lack of energy, vitality or interest.

External Parasites

FLEAS AND TICKS

Fleas and ticks are the primary external parasites to which dogs are vulnerable, and you should take steps to prevent your Yorkie from becoming host to these blood suckers. Don't, however, go overboard. A chemical strong enough to kill fleas and ticks is potentially dangerous to your dog as well. When misused, overused and combined, these products can be worse for your dog than the pests themselves. Here are some tips for prevention:

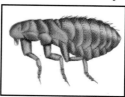

The flea is a die-hard pest.

- Keep your dog in maximum good health. Healthy dogs with strong immune systems are able to repel pests naturally.

- Avoid close contact with other dogs or outdoor cats. Fleas can easily jump from one animal to another.

- Learn when pests are in full force where you live. Avoid sandy, grassy and wooded areas during flea and tick season.

- Listen to old wives' tales. Scientific types insist they can't work, but many dog owners swear by such products as garlic, brewer's yeast, citrus rind, herbal preparations and even Avon Skin So Soft™ bath oil. True, they might not work, but then again they may; if they can't hurt, there's no reason not to try them.

Once you've got the problem, you have to get rid of it. Here are tips for killing fleas and ticks:

- Assess the situation. If your dog has three fleas or a tick from a day in the country, you can safely remove these with a flea shampoo and a pair of tweezers, respectively. Regular grooming and inspection will make sure you discover pests almost as soon as they land on your dog, when the problem is definitely manageable.

- If there are a lot of fleas, treat the dog, the house and the yard. Nothing else can possibly work. But keep in mind that you cannot treat your dog with the same products that you use on grass or carpeting. Ask your veterinarian for product recommendations and be sure to follow the label instructions to the letter!

- Attack the flea in all life stages: egg, larva and adult. There are different products specified for each stage, and none works for all three. Ask your veterinarian for recommendations of products to use on your dog, and follow instructions explicitly. If you think your premises and yard are infested, call an exterminator. *Note:* Keep your dog off treated areas for twenty-four hours.

FIGHTING FLEAS

Remember, the fleas you see on your dog are only part of the problem—the smallest part! To rid your dog and home of fleas, you need to treat your dog *and* your home. Here's how:

- Identify where your pet(s) sleep. These are "hot spots."

- Clean your pets' bedding regularly by vacuuming and washing.

- Spray "hot spots" with a non-toxic, long-lasting flea larvicide.

- Treat outdoor "hot spots" with insecticide.

- Kill eggs on pets with a product containing insect growth regulators (IGRs).

- Kill fleas on pets per your veterinarian's recommendation.

The seriousness of both flea and tick infestations should not be underestimated. A large number of fleas can actually kill a dog, especially one that is very young or aged. Each time one of them bites your Yorkie, it eats a drop or two of blood. When your dog is covered by hundreds of fleas, each of which bites him numerous times a day, the blood loss can actually be quite substantial. In addition, fleas can cause skin allergies and are the intermediary hosts of tapeworms, an internal parasite.

You should inspect your Yorkie thoroughly for ticks, especially where they tend to collect: in the ears, or in the hair at the base of the ear; in the armpits; and around the genitals. If you find a tick on your dog, remove it by first covering it with petroleum jelly. This

will suffocate the tick and force it to back out. Once this happens, you can then grab it with a pair of tweezers and kill it. If the tick doesn't back out, grab it with the tweezers and slowly pull it out with a twisting motion. It is

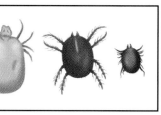

important not to pull too forcefully, as the head may separate from the body and remain in the dog's skin, likely causing the bite to become infected or form an abscess. It is also of utmost importance to use

Three types of ticks (l-r): the wood tick, brown dog tick and deer tick.

tweezers, not your fingers, when removing a tick. Ticks can carry diseases, including Lyme disease and Rocky Mountain spotted fever, so it's best to avoid direct contact with them whenever possible.

Internal Parasites

Roundworms Roundworms, probably the most common of the internal parasites, show up most frequently in puppies, although it is possible for adult dogs and even people to be infested. Since the worms are transmitted through feces, dogs often pick them up by sniffing feces

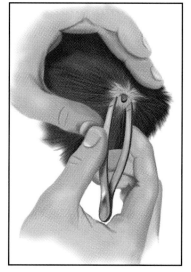

left behind by infected dogs. Because of the easy transmission of this parasite, it is always a good idea to make sure that feces left behind by both your dog and other dogs are picked up every day.

Use tweezers to remove ticks from your dog.

When treated early, roundworms should not turn into a serious health concern. However, a heavy infestation can severely affect your dog's health. The adult female roundworm can lay up to 200,000 eggs a day, which are then passed out with the dog's feces. Mature roundworms, which will also be passed during bowel movements, resemble strands of spaghetti, and can be eight to ten inches long. A puppy with an infestation of this type will usually have a pot belly, a thin appearance and a coat lacking shine and luster. The dog may also show signs of infestation in other ways: vomiting, sometimes bringing up worms; diarrhea; weight loss and an overall unhealthy look. Young puppies already infested at birth can die within two to three weeks, as severe dehydration will often accompany these symptoms.

Roundworms can be more dangerous in humans, so it is especially important both to see that your own surroundings are kept clean of animal waste and that you contact your veterinarian as soon as you suspect that your dog may be supporting the parasite.

Hookworms   Hookworms are reason for somewhat more alarm than roundworms. These bloodsucking parasites can cause anemia in both puppies and adults,

Common internal parasites (l-r): roundworm, whipworm, tapeworm and hookworm.

and their eggs are also passed through feces. These very hardy eggs can survive for long periods of time in sand or soil, even after the feces have been removed. Puppies are often infected through their mother's milk, but they can also enter the dog through the feet and the skin. The parasite burrows through the skin and migrates to the intestinal tract, where it attaches to the intestinal wall. Hookworms can also be acquired by humans through similar means, often through the skin of bare feet. It is therefore important to be cautious when walking barefoot in sandy or earthy areas where dogs are likely to defecate.

A dog infected with hookworms will usually pass a somewhat slimy stool, or have bloody diarrhea. Other symptoms may include weakness, pale gums, weight loss and dehydration. Take your dog to the veterinarian immediately if you suspect that he may have been infected with hookworms.

Tapeworms Diligent flea control is necessary to lessen the chances of tapeworm infection in your Yorkie. These, the second most common parasite in dogs, are usually acquired when the dog swallows a flea while chewing at himself to scratch a flea bite. The flea serves as an intermediate host for the parasite. After gaining access to the dog's system, the tapeworm will attach to the wall of the intestines and support itself by absorbing nutrients.

You will most likely notice that your dog has tapeworms when you see rice-like segments in your dog's stool, in the fur around the dog's rectal area and perhaps even on his bedding. Tapeworms are certainly not the most devastating of internal parasites, but they still warrant prompt veterinary attention. Usually one deworming will rid the dog of the infestation, but the next round of fleas will likely present the same problem. Keeping fleas under control is the only way to effectively rid your Yorkie of tapeworms completely.

Whipworms Whipworms, which feed on blood, live in the large intestines. These thread-like parasites are somewhat thicker at one end than at the other, and reach two to three inches in length at maturity. Their eggs are passed in feces, and once left behind in the soil, can survive for many years. An infected dog has usually picked the parasite up by digging and sniffing in infected soil, which can also be the source of infection for humans. Since the eggs can survive for such a long time, disinfecting your environment can be difficult. The most effective precautionary measures include cleaning dog runs and areas where dogs frequently defecate with a bleach and water mixture; wearing gloves when digging in soil likely to be infected; and being cautious about where you choose to walk barefoot, whether in the park, at the beach or even in your own yard.

Diagnosing a case of whipworms can be difficult since the worms do not release eggs into the stool every day. If you suspect that your dog might be infected, collect stool samples for several days in a row and take them to your veterinarian for analysis. Suspect infestation if

your dog has diarrhea, often bloody or watery, and if
he has a thin, anemic look with a poor coat. Severe
bowel problems and anemia usually result from these
parasites, so take your Yorkie to your veterinarian as
soon as you notice symptoms of this sort.

Heartworms   Dogs become infected by heartworms
when they are bitten by a mosquito that carries the
parasite. Adult heartworms live in the heart and lungs
of an infected dog, and their offspring (microfilaria)
circulate in the bloodstream. The likelihood that your
dog will become infected depends somewhat on the
climate in which you live. Areas that tend to be warm
and moist for most of the year will see an increased
population of mosquitoes, and will therefore see an
increased number of heartworm infections. Your veterinarian should be able to advise you on the risk
present in your particular area.

There are pills that you can give your dog to prevent
heartworm infection, but it's important to first make
sure that your dog isn't already infested. If he is,
giving the treatment will only worsen his condition
and may result in death. Always consult with your veterinarian before beginning any preventative care of
this nature.

The adult heartworm can cause severe illness and even
death due to congestive heart failure and/or emboli
(blood clots) in the lungs. Suspect heartworms if you
and your veterinarian see signs of liver problems,
coughing and weight loss. Heartworm infestation is
usually confirmed by X rays.

PROTOZOA

There are two protozoan diseases of concern to Yorkie
owners. A protozoan is a one-celled animal that finds
its way into a dog's system as a tiny cyst ingested with
contaminated feces. These cysts eventually wind up in
the lining of the bowel, where they mature.

Coccidia   As unpleasant as the idea may be, dogs
may sometimes eat their own feces or the feces of
other dogs. If those feces are contaminated with this

protozoan, the dog will become infected. Dogs affected by coccidia are most often puppies, who have been infected by their mothers before birth. While the disease is seen mostly in puppies, it is possible for adults to have it or to be carriers. Dogs can reinfect themselves by touching their own feces or that of other infected dogs, so good sanitation is the key to keeping you dog free of coccidia.

One of the first symptoms you are likely to see is a mucuslike diarrhea, sometimes containing blood. Other symptoms include: runny eyes and nose, coughs, dehydration, anemia, weight loss and weakness.

Giardia   This protozoan is common in wild animals and is often spread to domestic animals, and people, through contaminated drinking water. Your Yorkie may come down with a case of giardia if he's gone exploring through the woods, or other areas inhabited by wild animals, and has been drinking water from contaminated puddles. Diarrhea and bloody stools after a hiking or camping outing are usually the best indicators of an infection of this sort.

Infectious Diseases

The diseases listed below can all be prevented, to a certain extent, by vaccinating your Yorkie, starting when he's a puppy. Unfortunately, vaccinations are no guarantee that he will not get sick. Many factors govern how well a dog reacts to a vaccination, including the antibodies the dog got from his mother, how the dog's own immune system reacts to the vaccine and his general state of health. If you have any questions about vaccinations, call your veterinarian. He or she can answer your questions and recommend a vaccination schedule for your dog.

Distemper   Distemper is a very contagious viral disease that, unfortunately, has not been eradicated despite the use of vaccinations against it.

Dogs with distemper usually display the following symptoms: weakness, fever, discharge from the eyes and the nose, coughing, vomiting and diarrhea. While intravenous fluids and antibiotics may help an infected dog, this treatment is rarely successful; most dogs with distemper die.

Hepatitis Infectious canine hepatitis is a highly contagious virus that primarily attacks the liver but can also cause sever kidney damage. It is not related to the form of hepatitis that affects people. The virus is spread through contaminated saliva, mucus, urine or feces. Initial symptoms include depression, vomiting, abdominal pain, high fever and jaundice. Mild cases may be treated with intravenous fluids, antibiotics and even blood transfusions; however, the mortality rate is very high.

Coronavirus This virus is rarely fatal to adult dogs, although it is frequently fatal to puppies. The symptoms include vomiting, loss of appetite and a yellowish, watery stool that might contain mucus or blood. The stools carry the virus, which is highly contagious. Fluid or electrolyte therapy can alleviate the dehydration associated with diarrhea, but there is no treatment for the virus itself.

Parvovirus Parvo, as this disease is commonly known, is a devastating killer of puppies. A severe gastrointestinal virus, parvo attacks the inner lining of the intestines, causing bloody diarrhea with a distinct odor. In puppies under ten weeks of age, the virus also attacks the heart, causing death, often with no other symptoms. Parvo is so extremely contagious that it has swept through kennels and humane societies, causing multiple deaths in as little as forty-eight hours.

The gastroenteritis can be treated with fluid therapy and antibiotics; however, the virus moves rapidly, and

---

WHEN TO CALL THE VET

In any emergency situation, you should call your veterinarian immediately. You can make the difference in your dog's life by staying as calm as possible when you call and by giving the doctor or the assistant as much information as possible before you leave for the clinic. That way, the vet will be able to take immediate, specific action to remedy your dog's situation.

Emergencies include acute abdominal pain, suspected poisoning, snakebite, burns, frostbite, shock, dehydration, abnormal vomiting or bleeding, and deep wounds. You are the best judge of your dog's health, as you live with and observe him every day. Don't hesitate to call your veterinarian if you suspect trouble.

dehydration can lead to shock and death in a matter of hours.

Leptospirosis   This highly contagious bacterial disease is spread by the urine of infected wildlife. If your Yorkie sniffs at a bush that has been urinated on, or drinks from a contaminated stream, he may pick up this bacteria that causes either kidney disease or liver infection. Humans are also susceptible to infection by lepto.

Symptoms of lepto include fever, loss of appetite, possible diarrhea and jaundice. Antibiotics can be used to treat the disease, but the outcome is usually not good, due to the serious kidney and liver damage caused by the bacteria.

Tracheobronchitis   Commonly called "canine cough" or "kennel cough," this respiratory infection can be caused by any number of different viral or bacterial agents. These highly contagious, airborne agents can cause a variety of symptoms, including inflammation of the trachea, bronchi and lungs, as well as mild to severe coughing. Antibiotics may be prescribed to combat or prevent pneumonia, and a cough suppressant may quiet the cough. Fortunately, the disease is usually mild, and many dogs recover quickly without any treatment at all.

Rabies   Rabies is a highly infectious virus usually carried by wildlife, especially bats, raccoons and skunks. Any warm-blooded animals, including humans, may become infected, however. The virus is transmitted by saliva introduced to the animal through a bite or break in the skin. The virus then travels up to the brain and spinal cord and spreads throughout the body.

Behavior changes are the first sign of the disease. Nocturnal animals will come out during the day; fearful or shy animals will become bold and aggressive or friendly and affectionate. As the virus spreads, the animal will have trouble swallowing and will drool or salivate excessively. Paralysis and convulsions follow. There is no treatment; however, vaccinations are very effective and are available for people, as well as dogs.

Health Problems: Signs and Symptoms

Symptoms are not diseases. They are signs that something is wrong and should never be ignored. The "something" may be minor or it may be major. If you're not sure, it is always better to be too cautious and take your Yorkie to the veterinarian right away. It's such a relief to be told "It's nothing serious" that you won't even mind the time and money spent. On the other hand, delaying too long and then being told, "If we'd only seen him sooner . . . " can haunt your dreams forever. Here are common signs that something is wrong:

Constipation   If your Yorkie strains repeatedly without passing a stool, he is constipated. Not having a bowel movement one day is not constipation. If your Yorkie has a long coat, make sure that hair and stool have not become matted together, causing an external blockage.

Simple constipation in dogs is usually the result of inadequate fiber in the diet, not enough fat or not enough exercise. Eating bones or indigestible matter, such as grass, can also cause constipation. Try giving your Yorkie about a half-teaspoon of mineral oil mixed in with his food. If that doesn't work within a few hours, make an appointment to visit your veterinarian.

Coughing   Coughing can have a myriad of causes, virtually all of which need professional treatment. As previously mentioned in the "Genetic Defects" section, many Yorkies and other Toy dogs suffer from "collapsing trachea," where the windpipe is more flaccid than it should be and the sides collapse inward and stick, causing irritation and cough. The condition is permanent, but your veterinarian can advise you on different options. Two things that you can do are make sure your Yorkie is not overweight, and avoid putting any pressure on the windpipe (another reason I like to see a Yorkie in a harness rather than a leash).

Diarrhea   Frequent, loose and watery stools can also be caused by many different things. One or two loose movements may be the result of a minor upset; six or more should probably be taken seriously, as dehydration can result. Another factor to consider in how quickly you take your Yorkie to the vet is whether or not he's acting sick or has a fever. Uncomplicated diarrhea can be treated for a day by withholding all food for twelve hours, then feeding very bland food such as cooked chicken, boiled eggs or macaroni, and giving about a teaspoon of Kaopectate™ every six hours. If there's blood or mucous in the diarrhea, vomiting, fever or generalized sickness, take the dog to the veterinarian.

Frequent Urination   Frequent and "urgent" urination of scant amounts usually signals a bladder infection; you will need to slip a saucer under him to get a sample to take to the veterinarian. You may or may not see blood in the urine.

Limping   By careful observation, you should be able to tell which limb is hurting and, sometimes, why. Holding a foot up usually means there's something stuck on or between the pads. If the dog has just jumped or fallen from some high place, the cause is obvious, although the severity of the injury may not be.

Pacing/Panting   Mostly this is a sign of anxiety, although it can also accompany pain. Examine your Yorkie carefully and gently to see if you can find something that hurts. The Wee once went into a state of feverish pacing and panting, and when I put my hands on her, I was horrified to find that her abdomen was hugely distended and tight as a drum. Certain that she had bloat, a gravely serious condition that is caused when the stomach twists and traps gas inside, I rushed her to the Animal Medical Center in New York City. (I had never heard of a Toy dog having bloat, but I wasn't taking any chances.) On the ride in the car, I discovered that she had gas all right, but it definitely was able to escape! When it did, her anxiety escaped with it and within minutes she was completely back to normal. I still had the emergency staff check her out.

Pawing at the Mouth   Assuming the dog is not choking (unable to breathe), this sign invariably means there is something stuck in the mouth. Open the mouth gently if you can, if you can see the whole object you may be able to remove it yourself. Use extreme caution in removing anything that has penetrated the skin as it's very difficult to hold a Yorkie's head completely still; even if you can remove the object, it may need to be followed up by an antibiotic.

Rubbing at the Eye   Dogs rub both eyes persistently against the sofa or carpet when their eyes are generally itchy or irritated due to such things as smoke or allergies. But when they rub one eye frantically, or paw at it, they are in pain. Either there is something in that eye, or there is a scratch on the cornea. I consider this an emergency, as they can do a lot of damage to themselves until they get relief. Chances are they will not tolerate your looking around to see what the problem is.

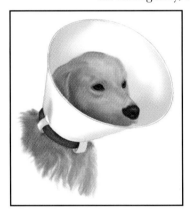

An Elizabethan collar keeps your dog from licking a fresh wound.

Scratching   Dogs scratch from fleas, mites and other things that bite; from dry skin; from shampoo residue; and from allergies of many kinds. If your Yorkie is scratching a particular body part, such as his ear, look there for the problem. Some dogs are very allergic to fleas, and even if the fleas (or single flea) are removed, the scratching goes on . . . and on. If a flea bath or regular shampoo, followed by thorough rinsing, doesn't seem to help, you'll need your veterinarian to investigate. Itchy skin is another condition that is thought to be exacerbated by an unwholesome lifestyle, over-processed foods, over-medication, injudicious use of pesticides and so on.

Shivering   Shivering and trembling can look similar but the circumstances, as well as the dog's expression and body language, can usually distinguish the two. A cold dog looks miserable, is usually wet and is probably trying to climb up your pant leg. A shivering dog who has other symptoms of illness, such as staggering or confusion, or who has just suffered some sort of trauma, needs emergency treatment. A trembling dog looks and acts fearful, with a tucked, cowering posture. This behavior is most often displayed in the veterinarian's office, so there's no need to take him there for evaluation! If you don't know why your Yorkie is trembling and there's any possibility that he might have ingested poison, this is obviously an emergency situation.

Vomiting Dogs vomit for many reasons, mostly dietary ones. Vomiting once or twice, without other signs of sickness or distress, can be treated at home. Withhold food and water for twelve hours, then offer very small meals of bland food and, if that stays down, repeat in four hours. Offer only minute amounts of water. If all goes well for twenty-four hours, feed normal portions of bland food for one more day just to be on the safe side. Frequent vomiting, unproductive retching or vomiting with blood, pain, fever or diarrhea need prompt veterinary attention.

Emergencies

Emergencies involving your dog are among life's most dreadful moments. The stakes are impossibly high, every second counts and the outcome often depends on you keeping a cool head. Nothing ever quite prepares you for a true emergency, but there are some things you can do ahead of time to improve your effectiveness in the event of a threat to the very life of your Yorkie.

A FIRST-AID KIT

Keep a canine first-aid kit on hand for general care and emergencies. Check it periodically to make sure liquids haven't spilled or dried up, and replace medications and materials after they're used. Your kit should include:

Activated charcoal tablets

Adhesive tape
(1 and 2 inches wide)

Antibacterial ointment
(for skin and eyes)

Aspirin (buffered or enteric coated, *not* Ibuprofen)

Bandages: Gauze rolls (1 and 2 inches wide) and dressing pads

Cotton balls

Diarrhea medicine

Dosing syringe

Hydrogen peroxide (3%)

Petroleum jelly

Rectal thermometer

Rubber gloves

Rubbing alcohol

Scissors

Tourniquet

Towel

Tweezers

Be clear about what an emergency is. An emergency is not determined by what happened, but by how your dog is reacting. In other words, a fall is not an emergency (The Wee once fell from the kitchen counter with no ill effects at all!); unconsciousness is the emergency. By definition, an emergency is any situation where immediate action is needed to prevent your dog from dying or suffering irreversible damage.

Know the location and telephone number of the nearest veterinarian or emergency clinic. This applies not

only to where you live but anywhere you may travel with your Yorkie.

Know how you will get there. If you don't drive, or don't have a car, think this through ahead of time and list the telephone numbers of several car services or animal taxis in your record book or by your telephone. Yorkie owners are fortunate that taxicab drivers usually do not object to transporting small dogs that can be carried. Even so, many will insist that the dog be inside a carrier.

Prepare a first-aid kit. (See sidebar for items to include in this kit.) Review the kit from time to time and replace out-of-date items. Also make sure nothing has spilled or evaporated. If your Yorkie travels with you in your car, have an identical kit for the car and for traveling with your dog.

Run your hands regularly over your dog to feel for any injuries.

Take a course in first aid. My veterinarian sponsored an after-hours first-aid clinic for his clients, demonstrating on live dogs. Ask your veterinarian if he or she would consider doing this. If a course of this sort is not available, a first-aid course for humans, while not as reassuring as one focused on pets, is certainly better than nothing.

According to the definition given above, there are only a handful of conditions that always call for an emergency response. That does not mean that you should not rush your Yorkie to the hospital, or at least call for guidance, whenever you are uncertain. But if one or more of the following symptoms appear, you should call ahead, then rush your dog to the nearest veterinarian or emergency clinic:

- Uncontrollable bleeding
- Extremely labored breathing
- Convulsions
- Sudden paralysis
- Shock
- Unconsciousness
- Continuous vomiting or diarrhea

There are many events that are likely to, or inevitably will, cause one or more of the emergency symptoms mentioned above. Sometimes a serious but undiagnosed illness is the cause, although it would be unlikely that you would not have seen other signs first. Following are some of the more common situations that send Yorkies to the emergency room. Note how many of them could be prevented with a little common sense!

Emergency Situations

Animal Encounters   With a dog as small as a Yorkie, almost any unfriendly encounter with another animal can be an emergency. For instance, if a larger dog grabs a Yorkie and shakes him, internal injuries can occur even if the skin isn't broken and nothing looks wrong. Have it checked out immediately. Other animal encounters that I would treat as an emergency include: bee stings; bites of any kind, including by insects you're not familiar with and certainly by such animals as bats, scorpions and snakes (see "Snakebite," below); cat scratches to the eye; porcupine quills anywhere; skunk spray to the eyes. If your Yorkie is bitten by an animal that you or he kills, wrap the animal up (without touching it directly) and take it with you.

External Bleeding   Bleeding in dogs is usually caused by cuts and bites, mostly from other dogs, or by accidents where limbs are broken and protrude through the skin. If your Yorkie is bleeding from an injury, attempt to stem the loss of blood. Bleeding from a cut should stop within five minutes or so. If it does not, or if bleeding is profuse, apply a pressure bandage. To make a pressure bandage, place a gauze pad or folded square of clean, absorbent material directly over the wound and apply firm pressure with your hand. Even if the bleeding stops, proceed to the veterinarian, as the wound probably will need sutures in order to heal properly.

Internal Bleeding   Bleeding of the internal organs, evidenced by blood in the urine, or by blood flowing from the nose, mouth or other orifices, typically follows trauma. In a dog as tiny as a Yorkie, internal injuries can be caused by a fall, by being run over (not only by cars but bicycles and, more currently, by runaway in-line skates) or by being shaken by a larger dog. Internal bleeding may not be visible, but is frequently indicated by difficult breathing, abdominal pain or shock (see "Shock," below). If none of the other emergency signs are present, cover the dog loosely for warmth and seek immediate help.

Make a temporary splint by wrapping the leg in firm casing, then bandaging it.

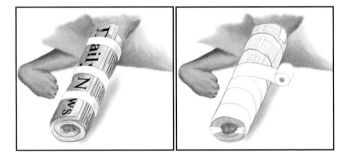

Broken Bones   Yorkies can suffer broken bones when they fall or are dropped from heights. I like to believe Yorkies are too smart to jump from heights higher than they can safely manage, but in the passion of the moment, I'm sure they might not always follow their better judgment. Suspect broken bones after an accident when the dog is in obvious pain and will not bear weight on one of his legs.

Broken bones can be very painful and your Yorkie may try to bite you. Muzzling is usually recommended (see diagram for instructions on how to make one), but I'd avoid using a muzzle unless necessary, since that kind of restraint might add to the Yorkie's distress. If the broken bone is protruding through the skin, put a clean bandage over the exposed bone ends and take the dog to a veterinarian immediately.

A **broken spine** is a true emergency. The dog may not appear to be in pain, but may show partial or complete paralysis. Moving a dog in this condition is risky, possibly causing further damage to the spinal cord and nerves. If this happens to your Yorkie, try to prevent the dog from moving at all. Pick the Yorkie up in such a way so as the back does not bend or twist; place him on a board or rigid surface and hold him in place, trying to keep him as calm as possible.

Applying abdominal thrusts can save a choking dog.

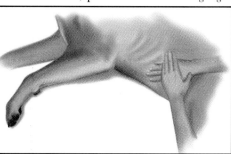

Choking   Dogs, like people, can choke to death if an object becomes lodged in the throat. The Yorkie will be totally panicked, pawing frantically at his mouth, possibly coughing and gagging. If the object is not promptly removed, unconsciousness and death will follow.

If there are two people available, you should grab the dog and head for the emergency clinic. While one drives, the other should care for the dog. If you can see the object at the back of the throat, try to dislodge it with a sweep of your finger. Take care not to push it further down. If the dog faints, open his mouth and apply enough pressure at the back of the neck to prevent the object from slipping further down the throat as you hook it with your fingers.

If you cannot see the object, you will have to try to force it out from the inside. First hold the Yorkie with his stomach along your forearm and with his head sloping downward. Strike him sharply between the shoulders with the heel of your hand a few times. If that doesn't work, hold the Yorkie with his back against you, head facing up. Make a fist with one hand and place it on the abdomen above the navel. Cover the fist with your other hand, and thrust sharply upward toward the Yorkie's ribs. Repeat as many times as necessary. Even if this doesn't work, keep speeding toward the clinic. Your Yorkie's survival will depend on his receiving the fastest possible attention by professional medical staff.

Dislocations   Yorkies and other Toys are prone to dislocations of the kneecap. As previously mentioned, this may be due to a genetic defect and if present, in mild or severe form, it will show up without regard to an accident. Yorkies who do not have the genetic condition may still dislocate joints rather than break bones when they fall or jump; you will need the veterinarian to determine which has happened. Dislocations need prompt veterinary attention. After twenty-four hours, dislocations may require surgery to repair.

Drowning   Yorkies are good swimmers, but they can get in trouble by leaping into bodies of water that they can't get out of, such as swimming pools or even bathtubs. If your dog dives in and gets in trouble, remove him from the water and suspend him upside down by the legs to allow the water to run out. Should the dog revive, you're very lucky, but you still need to take him to the veterinarian, as antibiotics may be needed to prevent pneumonia.

Depending on how long the Yorkie was without air, he may have only stopped breathing; however, his heart may have stopped as well. After a period of time without oxygen, the heart automatically stops. Since it is important not to massage the heart if it is still beating on its own, you should always feel for a pulse first when you think your Yorkie has stopped breathing (see "Pulse," p. 65). If indeed there is no pulse, proceed with either artificial respiration or with artificial respiration and heart massage (CPR), details for which follow. Meanwhile, rush the dog to a veterinarian. Do not cease your efforts, even if you see no response.

Heatstroke Heatstroke primarily occurs when a dog is left in a car in hot weather. Unlike humans, dogs cannot perspire; the only way they can cool themselves is by panting. This mechanism cannot keep up with the rapidly rising temperatures inside a car (or other enclosure, including a yard with no shade). If your Yorkie suffers from collapsing trachea or any other kind of airway problem, he is even more susceptible. Heat stroke is easy to recognize by the dog's frantic breathing, terrible anxiety, red tongue and thick saliva.

A dog suffering from heatstroke must be cooled immediately. Begin by taking him to an air-conditioned room and placing cold packs on the groin area. If the dog is staggering or appears near collapse, his entire body, excluding his head, needs to be immersed in cold—not freezing—water. If you have a thermometer handy, take his temperature. A reading over 106 degrees Fahrenheit is extremely critical. In any case, and even if the dog appears to recover, he should be taken immediately to a veterinarian for evaluation.

Poisoning Yorkies do not use good judgment when it comes to eating things they shouldn't. They can be poisoned by licking up antifreeze; eating poison that was set out for snails, slugs, mice or roaches; eating a poisonous plant or even grass that has been treated with a chemical—the list is almost endless.

If you suspect poisoning, call your emergency veterinary clinic and follow instructions while rushing the dog to the clinic. If you know exactly what the poison was, make sure you can relay the name; the clinic will be better able to advise you with that information. An alternative is to call the National Animal Poison Control Center at (800) 548-2423. The charge is $30 per case, payable by a major credit card.

Some of the many household substances harmful to your dog.

Few poisons have specific antidotes, so the first step in emergency treatment usually is to induce vomiting. Don't do this unless instructed to do so; depending on the poison, you could cause more damage. Agents that will induce vomiting are hydrogen peroxide three-percent solution, about a teaspoonful every ten minutes, repeated three times; or table salt, a half-teaspoonful placed far back in the mouth.

The next step usually is to administer a substance to dilute the poison or prevent it from being absorbed by the body. Three teaspoonfuls of activated charcoal mixed with water is an excellent absorbent. The third step is to give a laxative to eliminate the poison. After the charcoal has had half an hour to work, give Milk of Magnesia™, about one teaspoonful for every five pounds your Yorkie weighs. This will help clear the charcoal, containing the poison, from the intestines.

Keep in mind that you should undertake to treat your Yorkie only if you are not able to get immediate veterinary attention. It's always best to let the vet treat emergencies if possible. Don't, however, delay treatment for too long; time is of the essence when your dog is poisoned.

Remember: A poisonous substance on your Yorkie's coat will very likely soon be a poison in his stomach. You must remove it completely with soap and water. Do not use pet shampoos, as they may contain insecticides that will only add to the problem. Oily substances should first be soaked well with mineral or vegetable oil.

Shock   Shock occurs when some event disturbs the normal circulation of blood and oxygen to the tissues and organs. In dogs it is most often caused by trauma resulting in heavy blood loss, but can also be caused by heatstroke, poisoning, drowning, electric shock and other accidents. Shock is a life-threatening situation.

Suspect shock following an accident if the Yorkie appears depressed and unusually quiet. The gums will appear pale. The most important sign that shock is present is a slow *capillary refill time.* To check this, press firmly against the Yorkie's gums for a second or two, then release. The depression left by your finger will appear white. The time it takes to return to normal color is the capillary refill time. Anything over a second or two is abnormal; hold the dog with his head slightly lower than his heart, cover him lightly to preserve body heat and rush him to a veterinarian.

Snakebite Obviously, a snakebite is a potentially life-threatening attack to your Yorkie. Unless you're a snake expert, it's unlikely that you'll be able to positively identify the snake that bit him as poisonous or non-poisonous, so it's best to assume the worst. Examining the wound can provide some clues, however. Poisonous snakebites will show puncture wounds from the fangs, as well as horseshoe-shaped teeth marks.

If your dog has been bitten by a snake, restrain the dog and take him to the veterinarian as fast as you can. If you've managed to kill the snake, bring it along for the vet to identify. Meanwhile, it is very important to keep the dog as still as possible. He will be in extreme pain and may want to run away, but this will only cause the venom to circulate faster. Don't even let him walk. If the bite is on a leg, make a tourniquet (a tight bandage placed between the wound and the body). Take notice of the time and plan to loosen the tourniquet for thirty seconds every ten to fifteen minutes.

Next, take a knife or razor and cut two parallel cuts into the fang marks, about a quarter of an inch deep. Blood should ooze from the cuts; if it doesn't, loosen the tourniquet a little. Apply mouth suction (unless you have an open sore in your mouth) and then spit the blood out again. Do this continually for a half hour.

First Aid

The following are procedures for three emergency procedures mentioned in the preceding paragraphs. These procedures should be used in the time it takes to get your Yorkie to emergency veterinary care.

ARTIFICIAL RESPIRATION

1. Lay the dog on his right side on a flat, hard surface.

2. Open the mouth, extend the neck and pull the tongue forward, then close the mouth again and hold it shut.

3. Position your head so you can see the dog's chest, then put your mouth around the Yorkie's nose and blow in for about three seconds. Do not blow with a lot of force; as long as you can see the chest expand, you are blowing hard enough.

4. Release and watch the chest fall.

5. Repeat until the dog breathes on its own, or until you can turn him over to the veterinarian.

Do not practice Artificial Respiration on a dog that is breathing.

CPR

1. Lay the Yorkie on his right side on a flat, hard surface. If there are two people present and you can manage not to get in each other's way, have one perform artificial respiration and one massage the heart. If you are alone, you must do both, in alternating sets: one breath, six heart compressions and repeat.

2. To compress the heart, grasp the Yorkie's chest with your thumb on one side of the sternum (the breast bone) and your fingers on the other, just behind the elbow. Obviously you can't reach the heart directly, so in order to "massage" it, you have to squeeze it between the ribs and the breast bone.

3. Squeeze firmly at the rate of one compression a second.

4. Continue until the heart beats on its own, or until you are at the emergency clinic.

Do not practice CPR on a dog that is breathing or that has a pulse.

Senior Care

Toy dogs in general live longer than larger ones and seem to be "in their prime" at seven, eight and nine years old, when other dogs are already slowing down. Yorkies routinely live to be thirteen or fourteen, and frequently even longer. So assuming all is well with your Yorkie, the eighth, ninth and tenth years are a good time to start thinking about and planning for the changes that will gradually come.

EYES, EARS AND ACTIVITY

Signs of aging include failing eyesight and hearing, as well as greater sensitivity to temperature extremes. Your Yorkie may seem less eager to go outdoors and fling himself at the world; if so, it is more likely due to diminished sight or hearing than to arthritis or other joint problems that are common in large dogs of the same age.

When The Wee was around twelve, she began to hang back on some of her outings. It was only when I realized that her reluctance was limited to her late-night walk that it dawned on me that she might not be able to see after dark. Sure enough: She was more than happy to be active at that hour as long as we stayed in brightly lit areas. So unless you have reason to think your Yorkie does have stiff or painful joints, I would look for creative ways to keep him as physically active as he is able to be.

ROUTINES AND RITUALS

For the most part, your aging Yorkie will appreciate a minimum of change and upset in his life. If you have any choice in the matter, this is not the time to relocate, to go back to work full time or to add a new puppy or person to the household.

Feeding, walking, grooming and other schedules are also best left the same, though by all means, make any modifications that are appropriate. For instance, most Yorkies will appreciate less grooming and bathing. If you haven't already begun cutting the coat short, maybe it's time. The Wee never liked having her topknot tied up, so when she was middle aged, I gave in and kept the hair on top of her head cut short.

Keeping Up with Grooming

Now more than ever, it's important to keep up with regular brushing and combing, because your older Yorkie really will not like a marathon session to get out mats. Incidentally, having the whole coat clipped off with an electric clipper is not the simple remedy it sounds. Yorkies not accustomed to the noise and vibration of the clipper can be quite unhappy about it, and shaving off a badly matted coat is a long, arduous process with considerable risk of "clipper burn" to sensitive senior skin.

Attentive and thoughtful health care can help your Yorkie stay active even into his later years.

Caring for Teeth

Ongoing care of the teeth is also important. Many Yorkies have had many or most of their teeth removed by the time they reach senior status. It's important to remember that teeth are not ornamental; a dog with many missing teeth is limited in the kinds of foods he can eat and is denied the birthright of all dogs: to chew. (No teeth is still better than rotten teeth. Loose teeth and sore, swollen gums are not only painful, but the terrible odor is bound to cause you to keep your Yorkie at arm's length—just when he deserves more than ever to be held close and cherished.)

Making Allowances

Finally, as your Yorkie approaches the last lap of life, he may need a little extra help and consideration. Old dogs, like old humans, can get confused and forgetful sometimes, and should never be scolded for lapses in housetraining. And as Senior Sparky begins to spend more and more time sleeping, his preferred bed—even if it's yours—needs to be accessible.

For many years, The Wee was an impressive bed climber. She would approach at a run, launch herself through the air from an unlikely distance, land with her rear feet on the ledge where the mattress met the box spring and give an additional little kick that took her over the top. She did this a dozen times a day, usually bringing along a juicy chewstick, a favorite toy or a biscuit to bury in the pillows. The day came, however, when she was no longer able to get up on the bed. Being a dog, incapable of self-pity or regret, she wandered off to one of her other favorite spots. But Bill wasn't having any of that. In no time at all he'd built a ramp up to her "ledge," complete with carpeting. It took her two, maybe three, minutes to learn how to race up and down the ramp and she did so for an additional two years, even after she'd become almost completely blind. Of course, it was our pleasure to accommodate The Wee in her old age, trying to repay in small human ways the incalculable joy she'd brought into our lives.

FINAL KINDNESS

There are innumerable ways that a Yorkie's life can end. Probably the rarest is for him to go peacefully to sleep one night and just not wake up the next morning. Much more common is some combination of disease and disability, with or without distress, depression and discomfort. Your final responsibility to your Yorkie is to pay attention to the state of his well-being, day by day, so that you will know when life has become too great a burden for small shoulders to bear.

The decision to euthanize your Yorkie, to "put him to sleep," is yours to make, but you don't have to make it in a vacuum. Speak to your veterinarian. Ask whether or not the dog is in physical pain, whether or not recovery is possible and if so, what it will take and what the future quality of life may be. For example, modern veterinary medicine can work wonders with drugs, but if you've ever been on heavy medication for a period of time, you know there are often side-effects that can make you miserable in other ways. Consider whether your Yorkie is up to having a half-dozen pills forced down his throat each day or to making frequent trips back to the veterinarian's office. It may be hard to separate your needs from your Yorkie's at this point, but you must try. You don't want your old friend to suffer because you can't bear the thought of losing him. On the other hand, simply being old should never be a reason for euthanasia.

Euthanasia is performed by your veterinarian and consists of an overdose of anesthesia. The solution is administered by injection into a vein. The only pain is the prick of the needle and death comes in a matter of seconds.

I cannot imagine not accompanying a beloved dog on this final journey. If you know that he becomes terribly fearful at the veterinarian's office, ask the veterinarian for a tranquilizer or sedative that you can give ahead of time. Alternatively, a homeopath or herbalist can prescribe something to relieve stress without "zonking" the Yorkie. Ideally, you will have worked out these details ahead of time, perhaps even experimented with the effects of the particular preparation on your dog. The more prepared you feel, the calmer you will be, and that will be a comfort to your Yorkie.

FULL CIRCLE

The pain of losing your Yorkie, unfortunately, is a part of the experience of owning one of these delightful little dogs. Happily, Yorkies more often than not do reach a ripe old age, and at this point, old age is a lifetime away. In the next section of this book, you will learn many ways to make the most of the days and years ahead.

Your Happy, Healthy Pet

Your Dog's Name _____

Name on Your Dog's Pedigree (if your dog has one) _____

_____

Where Your Dog Came From _____

_____

Your Dog's Birthday _____

Your Dog's Veterinarian

    Name _____

    Address _____

    Phone Number _____

    Emergency Number _____

Your Dog's Health

    Vaccines

    type _____ date given _____

    type _____ date given _____

    type _____ date given _____

    type _____ date given _____

    Heartworm

    date tested _____ type used_____ start date _____

Your Dog's License Number_____

Groomer's Name and Number _____

Dogsitter/Walker's Name and Number_____

Awards Your Dog Has Won

    Award _____ date earned _____

    Award _____ date earned _____

part three

Enjoying
your
Dog

chapter 8

Basic
Training

by Ian Dunbar, Ph.D., MRCVS

Training is the jewel in the crown—the most important aspect of doggy husbandry. There is no more important variable influencing dog behavior and temperament than the dog's education: A well-trained, well-behaved and good-natured puppydog is always a joy to live with, but an untrained and uncivilized dog can be a perpetual nightmare. Moreover, deny the dog an education and she will not have the opportunity to fulfill her own canine potential; neither will she have the ability to communicate effectively with her human companions.

Luckily, modern psychological training methods are easy, efficient, effective and, above all, considerably dog-friendly and user-friendly.

Doggy education is as simple as it is enjoyable. But before you can have a good time play-training with your new dog, you have to learn what to do and how to do it. There is no bigger variable influencing the success of dog training than the *owner's* experience and expertise. *Before you embark on the dog's education, you must first educate yourself.*

Basic Training for Owners

Ideally, basic owner training should begin well *before* you select your dog. Find out all you can about your chosen breed first, then master rudimentary training and handling skills. If you already have your puppy-dog, owner training is a dire emergency—the clock is ticking! Especially for puppies, the first few weeks at home are the most important and influential days in the dog's life. Indeed, the cause of most adolescent and adult problems may be traced back to the initial days the pup explores her new home. This is the time to establish the *status quo*—to teach the puppydog how you would like her to behave and so prevent otherwise quite predictable problems.

In addition to consulting breeders and breed books such as this one (which understandably have a positive breed bias), seek out as many pet owners with your breed as you can find. Good points are obvious. What you want to find out are the breed-specific *problems,* so you can nip them in the bud. In particular, you should talk to owners with *adolescent* dogs and make a list of all anticipated problems. Most important, *test drive* at least half a dozen adolescent and adult dogs of your breed yourself. An 8-week-old puppy is deceptively easy to handle, but she will acquire adult size, speed and strength in just four months, so you should learn now what to prepare for.

Puppy and pet dog training classes offer a convenient venue to locate pet owners and observe dogs in action. For a list of suitable trainers in your area, contact the Association of Pet Dog Trainers (see chapter 13). You may also begin your basic owner training by observing other owners in class. Watch as many classes and test drive as many dogs as possible. Select an upbeat, dog-friendly, people-friendly, fun-and-games, puppydog pet training class to learn the ropes. Also, watch training videos and read training books. You must find out what to do and how to do it *before* you have to do it.

Principles of Training

Most people think training comprises teaching the dog to do things such as sit, speak and roll over, but even a 4-week-old pup knows how to do these things already. Instead, the first step in training involves teaching the dog human words for each dog behavior and activity and for each aspect of the dog's environment. That way you, the owner, can more easily participate in the dog's domestic education by directing her to perform specific actions appropriately, that is, at the right time, in the right place and so on. Training opens communication channels, enabling an educated dog to at least understand her owner's requests.

In addition to teaching a dog *what* we want her to do, it is also necessary to teach her *why* she should do what we ask. Indeed, 95 percent of training revolves around motivating the dog *to want to do* what we want. Dogs often understand what their owners want; they just don't see the point of doing it—especially when the owner's repetitively boring and seemingly senseless instructions are totally at odds with much more pressing and exciting doggy distractions. It is not so much the dog that is being stubborn or dominant; rather, it is the owner who has failed to acknowledge the dog's needs and feelings and to approach training from the dog's point of view.

The Meaning of Instructions

The secret to successful training is learning how to use training lures to predict or prompt specific behaviors—to coax the dog to do what you want *when* you want. Any highly valued object (such as a treat or toy) may be used as a lure, which the dog will follow with her eyes and nose. Moving the lure in specific ways entices the dog to move her nose, head and entire body in specific ways. In fact, by learning the art of manipulating various lures, it is possible to teach the dog to assume virtually any body position and perform any action. Once you have control over the expression of the dog's behaviors and can elicit any body position or behavior at will, you can easily teach the dog to perform on request.

Teach your dog words for each activity she needs to know, like down.

Tell your dog what you want her to do, use a lure to entice her to respond correctly, then profusely praise and maybe reward her once she performs the desired action. For example, verbally request "Tina, sit!" while you move a squeaky toy upwards and backwards over the dog's muzzle (lure-movement and hand signal), smile knowingly as she looks up (to follow the lure) and sits down (as a result of canine anatomical engineering), then praise her to distraction ("Gooood Tina!"). Squeak the toy, offer a training treat and give your dog and yourself a pat on the back.

Being able to elicit desired responses over and over enables the owner to reward the dog over and over. Consequently, the dog begins to think training is fun. For example, the more the dog is rewarded for sitting, the more she enjoys sitting. Eventually the dog comes to realize that, whereas most sitting is appreciated, sitting immediately upon request usually prompts especially enthusiastic praise and a slew of high-level rewards. The dog begins to sit on cue much of the time, showing that she is starting to grasp the meaning of the owner's verbal request and hand signal.

WHY COMPLY?

Most dogs enjoy initial lure-reward training and are only too happy to comply with their owners' wishes. Unfortunately, repetitive drilling without appreciative feedback tends to diminish the dog's enthusiasm until she eventually fails to see the point of complying anymore. Moreover, as the dog approaches adolescence she becomes more easily distracted as she develops other interests. Lengthy sessions with repetitive exercises tend to bore and demotivate both parties. If it's not fun, the owner doesn't do it and neither does the dog.

Integrate training into your dog's life: The greater number of training sessions each day and the *shorter* they are, the more willingly compliant your dog will

become. Make sure to have a short (just a few seconds) training interlude before every enjoyable canine activity. For example, ask your dog to sit to greet people, to sit before you throw her Frisbee and to sit for her supper. Really, sitting is no different from a canine "Please."

To train your dog, you need gentle hands, a loving heart and a good attitude.

Also, include numerous short training interludes during every enjoyable canine pastime, for example, when playing with the dog or when she is running in the park. In this fashion, doggy distractions may be effectively converted into rewards for training. Just as all games have rules, fun becomes training . . . and training becomes fun.

Eventually, rewards actually become unnecessary to continue motivating your dog. If trained with consideration and kindness, performing the desired behaviors will become self-rewarding and, in a sense, your dog will motivate herself. Just as it is not necessary to reward a human companion during an enjoyable walk in the park, or following a game of tennis, it is hardly necessary to reward our best friend—the dog—for walking by our side or while playing fetch. Human company during enjoyable activities is reward enough for most dogs.

Even though your dog has become self-motivating, it's still good to praise and pet her a lot and offer rewards once in a while, especially for a good job well done. And if for no other reason, praising and rewarding others is good for the human heart.

PUNISHMENT

Without a doubt, lure-reward training is by far the best way to teach: Entice your dog to do what you want and then reward her for doing so. Unfortunately, a human shortcoming is to take the good for granted and to moan and groan at the bad. Specifically, the dog's many good behaviors are ignored while the owner focuses on punishing the dog for making mistakes. In extreme cases, instruction is *limited* to punishing mistakes made by a trainee dog, child, employee or husband, even though it has been proven punishment training is notoriously inefficient and ineffective and is decidedly unfriendly and combative. It teaches the dog that training is a drag, almost as quickly as it teaches the dog to dislike her trainer. Why treat our best friends like our worst enemies?

Punishment training is also much more laborious and time consuming. Whereas it takes only a finite amount of time to teach a dog what to chew, for example, it takes much, much longer to punish the dog for each and every mistake. Remember, *there is only one right way!* So why not teach that right way from the outset?!

To make matters worse, punishment training causes severe lapses in the dog's reliability. Since it is obviously impossible to punish the dog each and every time she misbehaves, the dog quickly learns to distinguish between those times when she must comply (so as to avoid impending punishment) and those times when she need not comply, because punishment is impossible. Such times include when the dog is off leash and 6 feet away, when the owner is otherwise engaged (talking to a friend, watching television, taking a shower, tending to the baby or chatting on the telephone) or when the dog is left at home alone.

Instances of misbehavior will be numerous when the owner is away, because even when the dog complied in the owner's looming presence, she did so unwillingly. The dog was forced to act against her will, rather than molding her will to want to please. Hence, when the owner is absent, not only does the dog know she need not comply, she simply does not want to. Again, the trainee is not a stubborn vindictive beast, but rather the trainer has failed to teach. Punishment training invariably creates unpredictable Jekyll and Hyde behavior.

Trainer's Tools

Many training books extol the virtues of a vast array of training paraphernalia and electronic and metallic gizmos, most of which are designed for canine restraint, correction and punishment, rather than for actual facilitation of doggy education. In reality, most effective training tools are not found in stores; they come from within ourselves. In addition to a willing dog, all you really need is a functional human brain, gentle hands, a loving heart and a good attitude.

In terms of equipment, all dogs do require a quality buckle collar to sport dog tags and to attach the leash (for safety and to comply with local leash laws). Hollow chew toys (like Kongs or sterilized longbones) and a dog bed or collapsible crate are musts for housetraining. Three additional tools are required:

1. specific lures (training treats and toys) to predict and prompt specific desired behaviors;

2. rewards (praise, affection, training treats and toys) to reinforce for the dog what a lot of fun it all is; and

3. knowledge—how to convert the dog's favorite activities and games (potential distractions to training) into "life-rewards," which may be employed to facilitate training.

The most powerful of these is *knowledge*. Education is the key! Watch training classes, participate in training classes, watch videos, read books, enjoy play-training with your dog and then your dog will say "Please," and your dog will say "Thank you!"

Housetraining

If dogs were left to their own devices, certainly they would chew, dig and bark for entertainment and then no doubt highlight a few areas of their living space with sprinkles of urine, in much the same way we decorate by hanging pictures. Consequently, when we ask a dog to live with us, we must teach her *where* she may dig, *where* she may perform her toilet duties, *what* she may chew and *when* she may bark. After all, when left at home alone for many hours, we cannot expect the dog to amuse herself by completing crosswords or watching the soaps on TV!

Also, it would be decidedly unfair to keep the house rules a secret from the dog, and then get angry and punish the poor critter for inevitably transgressing rules she did not even know existed. Remember: Without adequate education and guidance, the dog will be forced to establish her own rules—doggy rules—and most probably will be at odds with the owner's view of domestic living.

Since most problems develop during the first few days the dog is at home, prospective dog owners must be certain they are quite clear about the principles of housetraining *before* they get a dog. Early misbehaviors quickly become established as the *status quo*—

becoming firmly entrenched as hard-to-break bad habits, which set the precedent for years to come. Make sure to teach your dog good habits right from the start. Good habits are just as hard to break as bad ones!

Ideally, when a new dog comes home, try to arrange for someone to be present as much as possible during the first few days (for adult dogs) or weeks for puppies. With only a little forethought, it is surprisingly easy to find a puppy sitter, such as a retired person, who would be willing to eat from your refrigerator and watch your television while keeping an eye on the newcomer to encourage the dog to play with chew toys and to ensure she goes outside on a regular basis.

POTTY TRAINING

To teach the dog where to relieve herself:

1. never let her make a single mistake;

2. let her know where you want her to go; and

3. handsomely reward her for doing so: "GOOOOOOD DOG!!!" liver treat, liver treat, liver treat!

Preventing Mistakes

A single mistake is a training disaster, since it heralds many more in future weeks. And each time the dog soils the house, this further reinforces the dog's unfortunate preference for an indoor, carpeted toilet. *Do not let an unhousetrained dog have full run of the house.*

When you are away from home, or cannot pay full attention, confine the dog to an area where elimination is appropriate, such as an outdoor run or, better still, a small, comfortable indoor kennel with access to an outdoor run. When confined in this manner, most dogs will naturally housetrain themselves.

If that's not possible, confine the dog to an area, such as a utility room, kitchen, basement or garage, where elimination may not be desired in the long run but as an interim measure it is certainly preferable to doing it all around the house. Use newspaper to cover the floor of the dog's day room. The newspaper may be used to soak up the urine and to wrap up and dispose of the feces. Once your dog develops a preferred spot for eliminating, it is only necessary to cover that part of the floor with newspaper. The smaller papered area may then be moved (only a little each day) towards the door to the outside. Thus the dog will develop the tendency to go to the door when she needs to relieve herself.

Never confine an unhousetrained dog to a crate for long periods. Doing so would force the dog to soil the crate and ruin its usefulness as an aid for housetraining (see the following discussion).

Teaching Where

In order to teach your dog where you would like her to do her business, you have to be there to direct the proceedings—an obvious, yet often neglected, fact of life. In order to be there to teach the dog *where* to go, you need to know *when* she needs to go. Indeed, the success of housetraining depends on the owner's ability to predict these times. Certainly, a regular feeding schedule will facilitate prediction somewhat, but there is nothing like "loading the deck" and influencing the timing of the outcome yourself!

The first few weeks at home are the most important and influential in your dog's life.

Whenever you are at home, make sure the dog is under constant supervision and/or confined to a small area. If already well trained, simply instruct the dog to lie down in her bed or basket. Alternatively, confine the dog to a crate (doggy den) or tie-down (a short, 18-inch lead that can be clipped to an eye hook in the baseboard near her bed). Short-term close confinement strongly inhibits urination and defecation, since the dog does not want to soil her sleeping area. Thus, when you release the puppydog each hour, she will definitely need to urinate immediately and defecate every third or fourth hour. Keep the dog confined to her doggy den and take her to her intended toilet area each hour, every hour and on the hour.

When taking your dog outside, instruct her to sit quietly before opening the door—she will soon learn to sit by the door when she needs to go out!

Teaching Why

Being able to predict when the dog needs to go enables the owner to be on the spot to praise and reward the dog. Each hour, hurry the dog to the intended toilet area in the yard, issue the appropriate instruction ("Go pee!" or "Go poop!"), then give the dog three to four minutes to produce. Praise and offer a couple of training treats when successful. The treats are important because many people fail to praise their dogs with feeling . . . and housetraining is hardly the time for understatement. So either loosen up and enthusiastically praise that dog: "Wuzzzer-wuzzer-wuzzer, hoooser good wuffer den? Hoooo went pee for Daddy?" Or say "Good dog!" as best you can and offer the treats for effect.

Following elimination is an ideal time for a spot of play-training in the yard or house. Also, an empty dog may be allowed greater freedom around the house for the next half hour or so, just as long as you keep an eye out to make sure she does not get into other kinds of mischief. If you are preoccupied and cannot pay full attention, confine the dog to her doggy den once more to enjoy a peaceful snooze or to play with her many chew toys.

If your dog does not eliminate within the allotted time outside—no biggie! Back to her doggy den, and then try again after another hour.

As I own large dogs, I always feel more relaxed walking an empty dog, knowing that I will not need to finish our stroll weighted down with bags of feces!

Beware of falling into the trap of walking the dog to get her to eliminate. The good ol' dog walk is such an enormous highlight in the dog's life that it represents the single biggest potential reward in domestic dogdom. However, when in a hurry, or during inclement weather, many owners abruptly terminate the walk the moment the dog has done her business. This, in effect, severely punishes the dog for doing the right thing, in the right place at the right time. Consequently, many dogs become strongly inhibited from eliminating outdoors because they know it will signal an abrupt end to an otherwise thoroughly enjoyable walk.

Instead, instruct the dog to relieve herself in the yard prior to going for a walk. If you follow the above instructions, most dogs soon learn to eliminate on cue. As soon as the dog eliminates, praise (and offer a treat or two)—"Good dog! Let's go walkies!" Use the walk as a reward for eliminating in the yard. If the dog does not go, put her back in her doggy den and think about a walk later on. You will find with a "No feces—no walk" policy, your dog will become one of the fastest defecators in the business.

If you do not have a backyard, instruct the dog to eliminate right outside your front door prior to the walk. Not only will this facilitate clean up and disposal of the feces in your own trash can but, also, the walk may again be used as a colossal reward.

CHEWING AND BARKING

Short-term close confinement also teaches the dog that occasional quiet moments are a reality of domestic living. Your puppydog is extremely impressionable during her first few weeks at home. Regular

confinement at this time soon exerts a calming influ-
ence over the dog's personality. Remember, once the
dog is housetrained and calmer, there will be a whole
lifetime ahead for the dog to enjoy full run of the
house and garden. On the other hand, by letting the
newcomer have unrestricted access to the entire household and allowing her to run willy-nilly, she will most
certainly develop a bunch of behavior problems in
short order, no doubt necessitating confinement later
in life. It would not be fair to remedially restrain and
confine a dog you have trained, through neglect, to
run free.

When confining the dog, make sure she always has an
impressive array of suitable chew toys. Kongs and sterilized longbones (both readily available from pet
stores) make the best chew toys, since they are hollow
and may be stuffed with treats to heighten the dog's
interest. For example, by stuffing the little hole at the
top of a Kong with a small piece of freeze-dried liver,
the dog will not want to leave it alone.

Remember, treats do not have to be junk food and
they certainly should not represent extra calories.
Rather, treats should be part of each dog's regular
daily diet: Some food
may be served in the
dog's bowl for break-
fast and dinner, some
food may be used as
training treats, and
some food may be
used for stuffing chew
toys. I regularly stuff
my dogs' many Kongs
with different shaped
biscuits and kibble.

*Make sure your
puppy has suit-
able chew toys.*

The kibble seems to fall out fairly easily, as do the
oval-shaped biscuits, thus rewarding the dog instanta-
neously for checking out the chew toys. The bone-
shaped biscuits fall out after a while, rewarding the dog
for worrying at the chew toy. But the triangular biscuits
never come out. They remain inside the Kong as lures,

maintaining the dog's fascination with her chew toy. To further focus the dog's interest, I always make sure to flavor the triangular biscuits by rubbing them with a little cheese or freeze-dried liver.

To teach come, call your dog, open your arms as a welcoming signal, wave a toy or a treat and praise for every step in your direction.

If stuffed chew toys are reserved especially for times the dog is confined, the puppydog will soon learn to enjoy quiet moments in her doggy den and she will quickly develop a chew-toy habit— a good habit! This is a simple *autoshaping* process; all the owner has to do is set up the situation and the dog all but trains herself— easy and effective. Even when the dog is given run of the house, her first inclination will be to indulge her rewarding chew-toy habit rather than destroy less-attractive household articles, such as curtains, carpets, chairs and compact disks. Similarly, a chew-toy chewer will be less inclined to scratch and chew herself excessively. Also, if the dog busies herself as a recreational chewer, she will be less inclined to develop into a recreational barker or digger when left at home alone.

Stuff a number of chew toys whenever the dog is left confined and remove the extra-special-tasting treats when you return. Your dog will now amuse herself with her chew toys before falling asleep and then resume playing with her chew toys when she expects you to return. Since most owner-absent misbehavior happens right after you leave and right before your expected return, your puppydog will now be conveniently preoccupied with her chew toys at these times.

Come and Sit

Most puppies will happily approach virtually anyone, whether called or not; that is, until they collide with adolescence and develop other more important doggy interests, such as sniffing a multiplicity of exquisite odors on the grass. Your mission, Mr./Ms. Owner, is to teach and reward the pup for coming reliably, willingly and happily when called—and you have just three months to get it done. Unless adequately reinforced, your puppy's tendency to approach people will self-destruct by adolescence.

Call your dog ("Tina, come!"), open your arms (and maybe squat down) as a welcoming signal, waggle a treat or toy as a lure and reward the puppydog when she comes running. Do not wait to praise the dog until she reaches you—she may come 95 percent of the way and then run off after some distraction. Instead, praise the dog's *first* step towards you and continue praising enthusiastically for *every* step she takes in your direction.

When the rapidly approaching puppy dog is three lengths away from impact, instruct her to sit ("Tina, sit!") and hold the lure in front of you in an outstretched hand to prevent her from hitting you midchest and knocking you flat on your back! As Tina decelerates to nose the lure, move the treat upwards and backwards just over her muzzle with an upwards motion of your extended arm (palm-upwards). As the dog looks up to follow the lure, she will sit down (if she jumps up, you are holding the lure too high). Praise the dog for sitting. Move backwards and call her again. Repeat this many times over, always praising when Tina comes and sits; on occasion, reward her.

For the first couple of trials, use a training treat both as a lure to entice the dog to come and sit and as a reward for doing so. Thereafter, try to use different items as lures and rewards. For example, lure the dog with a Kong or Frisbee but reward her with a food treat. Or lure the dog with a food treat but pat her and throw a tennis ball as a reward. After just a few repetitions, dispense with the lures and rewards; the dog will begin to respond willingly to your verbal requests and hand signals just for the prospect of praise from your heart and affection from your hands.

Instruct every family member, friend and visitor how to get the dog to come and sit. Invite people over for a series of pooch parties; do not keep the pup a secret— let other people enjoy this puppy, and let the pup enjoy other people. Puppydog parties are not only fun, they easily attract a lot of people to help *you* train *your* dog. Unless you teach your dog how to meet people, that is, to sit for greetings, no doubt the dog will resort to jumping up. Then you and the visitors will get annoyed, and the dog will be punished. This is not fair. *Send out those invitations for puppy parties and teach your dog to be mannerly and socially acceptable.*

Even though your dog quickly masters obedient recalls in the house, her reliability may falter when playing in the backyard or local park. Ironically, it is *the owner* who has unintentionally trained the dog *not* to respond in these instances. By allowing the dog to play and run around and otherwise have a good time, but then to call the dog to put her on leash to take her home, the dog quickly learns playing is fun but training is a drag. Thus, playing in the park becomes a severe distraction, which works against training. Bad news!

Instead, whether playing with the dog off leash or on leash, request her to come at frequent intervals—say, every minute or so. On most occasions, praise and pet the dog for a few seconds while she is sitting, then tell her to go play again. For especially fast recalls, offer a couple of training treats and take the time to praise and pet the dog enthusiastically before releasing her. The dog will learn that coming when called is not necessarily the end of the play session, and neither is it the end of the world; rather, it signals an enjoyable, quality time-out with the owner before resuming play once more. In fact, playing in the park now becomes a very effective life-reward, which works to facilitate training by reinforcing each obedient and timely recall. Good news!

Sit, Down, Stand and Rollover

Teaching the dog a variety of body positions is easy for owner and dog, impressive for spectators and extremely useful for all. Using lure-reward techniques, it is possible to train several positions at once to verbal commands or hand signals (which impress the socks off onlookers).

Sit and **down**—the two control commands—prevent or resolve nearly a hundred behavior problems. For example, if the dog happily and obediently sits or lies down when requested, she cannot jump on visitors, dash out the front door, run around and chase her tail, pester other dogs, harass cats or annoy family, friends or strangers. Additionally, "Sit" or "Down" are the best emergency commands for off-leash control.

It is easier to teach and maintain a reliable sit than maintain a reliable recall. *Sit* is the purest and simplest of commands—either the dog is sitting or she is not. If there is any change of circumstances or potential danger in the park, for example, simply instruct the dog to sit. If she sits, you have a number of options: Allow the dog to resume playing when she is safe, walk up and put the dog on leash or call the dog. The dog will be much more likely to come when called if she has already acknowledged her compliance by sitting. If the dog does not sit in the park—train her to!

Stand and *rollover-stay* are the two positions for examining the dog. Your veterinarian will love you to distraction if you take a little time to teach the dog to stand still and roll over and play possum. Also, your vet bills will be smaller because it will take the veterinarian less time to examine your dog. The rollover-stay is an especially useful command and is really just a variation of the down-stay: Whereas the dog lies prone in the traditional down, she lies supine in the rollover-stay.

As with teaching come and sit, the training techniques to teach the dog to assume all other body positions on cue are user-friendly and dog-friendly. Simply give the appropriate request, lure the dog into the desired body position using a training treat or toy and then *praise* (and maybe reward) the dog as soon as she complies. Try not to touch the dog to get her to respond. If you teach the dog by guiding her into position, the dog will quickly learn that rump-pressure means sit, for example, but as yet you still have no control over your dog if she is just 6 feet away. It will still be necessary to teach the dog to sit on request. So do not make training a time-consuming two-step process; instead, teach the dog to sit to a verbal request or hand signal from the outset. Once the dog sits willingly when requested, by all means use your hands to pet the dog when she does so.

To teach **down** when the dog is already sitting, say "Tina, down!," hold the lure in one hand (palm down) and lower that hand to the floor between the dog's forepaws. As the dog lowers her head to follow the lure, slowly move the lure away from the dog just a fraction (in front of her paws). The dog will lie down as she stretches her nose forward to follow the lure. Praise the dog when she does so. If the dog stands up, you pulled the lure away too far and too quickly.

When teaching the dog to lie down from the standing position, say "Down" and lower the lure to the floor as before. Once the dog has lowered her forequarters and assumed a play bow, gently and slowly move the lure *towards* the dog between her forelegs. Praise the dog as soon as her rear end plops down.

After just a couple of trials it will be possible to alternate sits and downs and have the dog energetically perform doggy push-ups. Praise the dog a lot, and after half a dozen or so push-ups reward the dog with a training treat or toy. You will notice the more energetically you move your arm—upwards (palm up) to get the dog to sit, and downwards (palm down) to get the dog to lie down—the more energetically the dog responds to your requests. Now try training the dog in silence and you will notice she has also learned to respond to hand signals. Yeah! Not too shabby for the first session.

To teach **stand** from the sitting position, say "Tina, stand," slowly move the lure half a dog-length away from the dog's nose, keeping it at nose level, and praise the dog as she stands to follow the lure. As soon

Using a food lure to teach sit, down and stand. 1) "Phoenix, sit." 2) Hand palm upwards, move lure up and back over dog's muzzle. 3) "Good sit, Phoenix!" 4) "Phoenix, down." 5) Hand palm downwards, move lure down to lie between dog's forepaws. 6) "Phoenix, off. Good down, Phoenix!" 7) "Phoenix, sit!" 8) Palm upwards, move lure up and back, keeping it close to dog's muzzle. 9) "Good sit, Phoenix!"

10) *"Phoenix, stand!" 11) Move lure away from dog at nose height, then lower it a tad. 12) "Phoenix, off! Good stand, Phoenix!" 13) "Phoenix, down!" 14) Hand palm downwards, move lure down to lie between dog's forepaws. 15) "Phoenix, off! Good down-stay, Phoenix!" 16) "Phoenix, stand!" 17) Move lure away from dog's muzzle up to nose height. 18) "Phoenix, off! Good stand-stay, Phoenix. Now we'll make the vet and groomer happy!"*

as the dog stands, lower the lure to just beneath the dog's chin to entice her to look down; otherwise she will stand and then sit immediately. To prompt the dog to stand from the down position, move the lure half a dog-length upwards and away from the dog, holding the lure at standing nose height from the floor.

Teaching *rollover* is best started from the down position, with the dog lying on one side, or at least with both hind legs stretched out on the same side. Say "Tina, bang!" and move the lure backwards and alongside the dog's muzzle to her elbow (on the side of her outstretched hind legs). Once the dog looks to the side and backwards, very slowly move the lure upwards to the dog's shoulder and backbone. Tickling the dog in the goolies (groin area) often invokes a reflex-raising of the hind leg as an appeasement gesture, which facilitates the tendency to roll over. If you move the lure too quickly and the dog jumps into the standing position, have patience and start again. As soon as the dog rolls onto her back, keep the lure stationary and mesmerize the dog with a relaxing tummy rub.

To teach *rollover-stay* when the dog is standing or moving, say "Tina, bang!" and give the appropriate hand signal (with index finger pointed and thumb cocked in true Sam Spade fashion), then in one fluid movement lure her to first lie down and then rollover-stay as above.

Teaching the dog to *stay* in each of the above four positions becomes a piece of cake after first teaching the dog not to worry at the toy or treat training lure. This is best accomplished by hand feeding dinner kibble. Hold a piece of kibble firmly in your hand and softly instruct "Off!" Ignore any licking and slobbering *for however long the dog worries at the treat,* but say "Take it!" and offer the kibble *the instant* the dog breaks contact with her muzzle. Repeat this a few times, and then up the ante and insist the dog remove her muzzle for one whole second before offering the kibble. Then progressively refine your criteria and have the dog not touch your hand (or treat) for longer and longer periods on each trial, such as for two seconds, four seconds, then six, ten, fifteen, twenty, thirty seconds and so on.

The dog soon learns: (1) worrying at the treat never gets results, whereas (2) noncontact is often rewarded after a variable time lapse.

Teaching *"Off!"* has many useful applications in its own right. Additionally, instructing the dog not to touch a training lure often produces spontaneous and magical stays. Request the dog to stand-stay, for example, and not to touch the lure. At first set your sights on a short two-second stay before rewarding the dog. (Remember, every long journey begins with a single step.) However, on subsequent trials, gradually and progressively increase the length of stay required to receive a reward. In no time at all your dog will stand calmly for a minute or so.

Relevancy Training

Once you have taught the dog what you expect her to do when requested to come, sit, lie down, stand, roll-over and stay, the time is right to teach the dog *why* she should comply with your wishes. The secret is to have many (*many*) extremely short training interludes (two to five seconds each) at numerous (*numerous*) times during the course of the dog's day. Especially work with the dog immediately *before* the dog's good times and *during* the dog's good times. For example, ask your dog to sit and/or lie down each time before opening doors, serving meals, offering treats and tummy rubs; ask the dog to perform a few controlled doggy push-ups before letting her off leash or throwing a tennis ball; and perhaps request the dog to sit-down-sit-stand-down-stand-rollover before inviting her to cuddle on the couch.

Similarly, request the dog to sit many times during play or on walks, and in no time at all the dog will be only too pleased to follow your instructions because she has learned that a compliant response heralds all sorts of goodies. Basically all you are trying to teach the dog is how to say please: "Please throw the tennis ball. Please may I snuggle on the couch."

Remember, it is important to keep training interludes short and to have many short sessions each and every day. The shortest (and most useful) session comprises asking the dog to sit and then go play during a play session. When trained this way, your dog will soon associate training with good times. In fact, the dog may be unable to distinguish between training and good times and, indeed, there should be no distinction. The warped concept that training involves forcing the dog to comply and/or dominating her will is totally at odds with the picture of a truly well-trained dog. In reality, enjoying a game of training with a dog is no different from enjoying a game of backgammon or tennis with a friend; and walking with a dog should be no different from strolling with a spouse, or with buddies on the golf course.

Walk by Your Side

Many people attempt to teach a dog to heel by putting her on a leash and physically correcting the dog when she makes mistakes. There are a number of things seriously wrong with this approach, the first being that most people do not want precision heeling; rather, they simply want the dog to follow or walk by their side. Second, when physically restrained during "training," even though the dog may grudgingly mope by your side when "handcuffed" on leash, let's see what happens when she is off leash. History! The dog is in the next county because she never enjoyed walking with you on leash and you have no control over her off leash. So let's just teach the dog off leash from the outset to *want* to walk with us. Third, if the dog has not been trained to heel, it is a trifle hasty to think about punishing the poor dog for making mistakes and breaking heeling rules she didn't even know existed. This is simply not fair! Surely, if the dog had been adequately taught how to heel, she would seldom make mistakes and hence there would be no need to correct the dog. Remember, each mistake and each correction (punishment) advertise the trainer's inadequacy, not the dog's. The dog is not stubborn, she is not stupid and she is not bad. Even if she were, she would still require training, so let's train her properly.

Let's teach the dog to *enjoy* following us and to *want* to walk by our side off leash. Then it will be easier to teach high-precision off-leash heeling patterns if desired. Before going on outdoor walks, it is necessary to teach the dog not to pull. Then it becomes easy to teach on-leash walking and heeling because the dog already wants to walk with you, she is familiar with the desired walking and heeling positions and she knows not to pull.

FOLLOWING

Start by training your dog to follow you. Many puppies will follow if you simply walk away from them and maybe click your fingers or chuckle. Adult dogs may require additional enticement to stimulate them to follow, such as a training lure or, at the very least, a lively trainer. To teach the dog to follow: (1) keep walking and (2) walk away from the dog. If the dog attempts to lead or lag, change pace; slow down if the dog forges too far ahead, but speed up if she lags too far behind. Say "Steady!" or "Easy!" each time before you slow down and "Quickly!" or "Hustle!" each time before you speed up, and the dog will learn to change pace on cue. If the dog lags or leads too far, or if she wanders right or left, simply walk quickly in the opposite direction and maybe even run away from the dog and hide.

Practicing is a lot of fun; you can set up a course in your home, yard or park to do this. Indoors, entice the dog to follow upstairs, into a bedroom, into the bathroom, downstairs, around the living room couch, zigzagging between dining room chairs and into the kitchen for dinner. Outdoors, get the dog to follow around park benches, trees, shrubs and along walkways and lines in the grass. (For safety outdoors, it is advisable to attach a long line on the dog, but never exert corrective tension on the line.)

Remember, following has a lot to do with attitude—*your* attitude! Most probably your dog will *not* want to follow Mr. Grumpy Troll with the personality of wilted lettuce. Lighten up—walk with a jaunty step, whistle a happy tune, sing, skip and tell jokes to your dog and she will be right there by your side.

BY YOUR SIDE

It is smart to train the dog to walk close on one side or the other—either side will do, your choice. When walking, jogging or cycling, it is generally bad news to have the dog suddenly cut in front of you. In fact, I train my dogs to walk "By my side" and "Other side"—both very useful instructions. It is possible to position the dog fairly accurately by looking to the appropriate side and clicking your fingers or slapping your thigh on that side. A precise positioning may be attained by holding a training lure, such as a chew toy, tennis ball or food treat. Stop and stand still several times throughout the walk, just as you would when window shopping or meeting a friend. Use the lure to make sure the dog slows down and stays close whenever you stop.

When teaching the dog to heel, we generally want her to sit in heel position when we stop. Teach heel

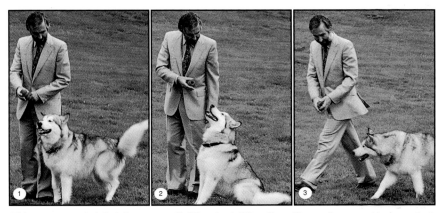

Using a toy to teach sit-heel-sit sequences: 1) "Phoenix, sit!" Standing still, move lure up and back over dog's muzzle . . . 2) to position dog sitting in heel position on your left side. 3) Say "Phoenix, heel!" and walk ahead, wagging lure in left hand. Change lure to right hand in preparation for sit signal. Say "Sit" and then . . .

position at the standstill and the dog will learn that the default heel position is sitting by your side (left or right—your choice, unless you wish to compete in obedience trials, in which case the dog must heel on the left).

Several times a day, stand up and call your dog to come and sit in heel position—"Tina, heel!" For example, instruct the dog to come to heel each time there are commercials on TV, or each time you turn a page of a novel, and the dog will get it in a single evening.

Practice straight-line heeling and turns separately. With the dog sitting at heel, teach her to turn in place. After each quarter-turn, half-turn or full turn in place, lure the dog to sit at heel. Now it's time for short straight-line heeling sequences, no more than a few steps at a time. Always think of heeling in terms of sit-heel-sit sequences—start and end with the dog in position and do your best to keep her there when moving. Progressively increase the number of steps in each sequence. When the dog remains close for 20 yards of straight-line heeling, it is time to add a few turns and then sign up for a happy-heeling obedience class to get some advice from the experts.

4) use hand signal to lure dog to sit as you stop. Eventually, dog will sit automatically at heel whenever you stop. 5) "Good dog!"

No Pulling on Leash

You can start teaching your dog not to pull on leash anywhere—in front of the television or outdoors—but regardless of location, you must not take a single step with tension in the leash. For a reason known only to dogs, even just a couple of paces of pulling on leash is intrinsically motivating and diabolically rewarding. Instead, attach the leash to the dog's collar, grasp the other end firmly with both hands held close to your chest, and stand still—do not budge an inch. Have somebody watch you with a stopwatch to time your progress, or else you will never believe this will work and so you will not even try the exercise, and your shoulder and the dog's neck will be traumatized for years to come.

Stand still and wait for the dog to stop pulling, and to sit and/or lie down. All dogs stop pulling and sit eventually. Most take only a couple of minutes; the all-time record is 22½ minutes. Time how long it takes. Gently praise the dog when she stops pulling, and as soon as she sits, enthusiastically praise the dog and take just one step forward, then immediately stand still. This single step usually demonstrates the ballistic reinforcing nature of pulling on leash; most dogs explode to the end of the leash, so be prepared for the strain. Stand firm and wait for the dog to sit again. Repeat this half a dozen times and you will probably notice a progressive reduction in the force of the dog's one-step explosions and a radical reduction in the time it takes for the dog to sit each time.

As the dog learns "Sit we go" and "Pull we stop," she will begin to walk forward calmly with each single step and automatically sit when you stop. Now try two steps before you stop. Wooooooo! Scary! When the dog has mastered two steps at a time, try for three. After each success, progressively increase the number of steps in the sequence: try four steps and then six, eight, ten and twenty steps before stopping. Congratulations! You are now walking the dog on leash.

Whenever walking with the dog (off leash or on leash), make sure you stop periodically to practice a few position commands and stays before instructing the dog to "Walk on!" (Remember, you want the dog to be compliant everywhere, not just in the kitchen when her dinner is at hand.) For example, stopping every 25 yards to briefly train the dog amounts to over 200 training interludes within a single 3-mile stroll. And each training session is in a different location. You will not believe the improvement within just the first mile of the first walk.

To put it another way, integrating training into a walk offers 200 separate opportunities to use the continuance of the walk as a reward to reinforce the dog's education. Moreover, some training interludes may comprise continuing education for the dog's walking skills: Alternate short periods of the dog walking calmly by your side with periods when the dog is allowed to sniff and investigate the environment. Now sniffing odors on the grass and meeting other dogs become rewards which reinforce the dog's calm and mannerly demeanor. Good Lord! Whatever next? Many enjoyable walks together of course. Happy trails!

THE IMPORTANCE OF TRICKS

Nothing will improve a dog's quality of life better than having a few tricks under her belt. Teaching any trick expands the dog's vocabulary, which facilitates communication and improves the owner's control. Also, specific tricks help prevent and resolve specific behavior problems. For example, by teaching the dog to fetch her toys, the dog learns carrying a toy makes the owner happy and, therefore, will be more likely to chew her toy than other inappropriate items.

More important, teaching tricks prompts owners to lighten up and train with a sunny disposition. Really, tricks should be no different from any other behaviors we put on cue. But they are. When teaching tricks, owners have a much sweeter attitude, which in turn motivates the dog and improves her willingness to comply. The dog feels tricks are a blast, but formal commands are a drag. In fact, tricks are so enjoyable, they may be used as rewards in training by asking the dog to come, sit and down-stay and then rollover for a tummy rub. Go on, try it: Crack a smile and even giggle when the dog promptly and willingly lies down and stays.

Most important, performing tricks prompts onlookers to smile and giggle. Many people are scared of dogs, especially large ones. And nothing can be more off-putting for a dog than to be constantly confronted by strangers who don't like her because of her size or the way she looks. Uneasy people put the dog on edge, causing her to back off and bark, only frightening people all the more. And so a vicious circle develops, with the people's fear fueling the dog's fear *and vice versa.* Instead, tie a pink ribbon to your dog's collar and practice all sorts of tricks on walks and in the park, and you will be pleasantly amazed how it changes people's attitudes toward your friendly dog. The dog's repertoire of tricks is limited only by the trainer's imagination. Below I have described three of my favorites:

SPEAK AND SHUSH

The training sequence involved in teaching a dog to bark on request is no different from that used when training any behavior on cue: request—lure—response—reward. As always, the secret of success lies in finding an effective lure. If the dog always barks at the doorbell, for example, say "Rover, speak!", have an accomplice ring the doorbell, then reward the dog for barking. After a few woofs, ask Rover to "Shush!", waggle a food treat under her nose (to entice her to sniff and thus to shush), praise her when quiet and eventually offer the treat as a reward. Alternate "Speak" and "Shush," progressively increasing the length of shush-time between each barking bout.

PLAY BOW

With the dog standing, say "Bow!" and lower the food lure (palm upwards) to rest between the dog's forepaws. Praise as the dog lowers her forequarters and sternum to the ground (as when teaching the down), but then lure the dog to stand and offer the treat. On successive trials, gradually increase the length of time the dog is required to remain in the play bow posture in order to gain a food reward. If the dog's rear end collapses into a down, say nothing and offer no reward; simply start over.

BE A BEAR

With the dog sitting backed into a corner to prevent her from toppling over backwards, say "Be a bear!" With bent paw and palm down, raise a lure upwards and backwards along the top of the dog's muzzle. Praise the dog when she sits up on her haunches and offer the treat as a reward. To prevent the dog from standing on her hind legs, keep the lure closer to the dog's muzzle. On each trial, progressively increase the length of time the dog is required to sit up to receive a food reward. Since lure-reward training is so easy, teach the dog to stand and walk on her hind legs as well!

Teaching "Be a Bear"

chapter 9

Getting

Active

with your Dog

by Bardi McLennan

Once you and your dog have graduated from basic obedience training and are beginning to work together as a team, you can take part in the growing world of dog activities. There are so many fun things to do with your dog! Just remember, people and dogs don't always learn at the same pace, so don't be upset if you (or your dog) need more than two basic training courses before your team becomes operational. Even smart dogs don't go straight to college from kindergarten!

Just as there are events geared to certain types of dogs, so there are ones that are more appealing to certain types of people. In some activities, you give the commands and your dog does the work (upland game hunting is one example), while in others, such as agility, you'll both get a workout. You may want to aim for prestigious titles to add to your dog's name, or you may want nothing more than the sheer enjoyment of being around other people and their dogs. Passive or active, participation has its own rewards.

Consider your dog's physical capabilities when looking into any of the canine activities. It's easy to see that a Basset Hound is not built for the racetrack, nor would a Chihuahua be the breed of choice for pulling a sled. A loyal dog will attempt almost anything you ask him to do, so it is up to you to know your dog's limitations. A dog must be physically sound in order to compete at any level in athletic activities, and being mentally sound is a definite plus. Advanced age, however, may not be a deterrent. Many dogs still hunt and herd at ten or twelve years of age. It's entirely possible for dogs to be "fit at 50." Take your dog for a checkup, explain to your vet the type of activity you have in mind and be guided by his or her findings.

All dogs seem to love playing flyball.

You needn't be restricted to breed-specific sports if it's only fun you're after. Certain AKC activities are limited to designated breeds; however, as each new trial, test or sport has grown in popularity, so has the variety of breeds encouraged to participate at a fun level.

But don't shortchange your fun, or that of your dog, by thinking only of the basic function of her breed. Once a dog has learned how to learn, she can be taught to do just about anything as long as the size of the dog is right for the job and you both think it is fun and rewarding. In other words, you are a team.

To get involved in any of the activities detailed in this chapter, look for the names and addresses of the organizations that sponsor them in Chapter 13. You can also ask your breeder or a local dog trainer for contacts.

You can compete in obedience trials with a well trained dog.

Official American Kennel Club Activities

The following tests and trials are some of the events sanctioned by the AKC and sponsored by various dog clubs. Your dog's expertise will be rewarded with impressive titles. You can participate just for fun, or be competitive and go for those awards.

OBEDIENCE

Training classes begin with pups as young as three months of age in kindergarten puppy training, then advance to pre-novice (all exercises on lead) and go on to novice, which is where you'll start off-lead work. In obedience classes dogs learn to sit, stay, heel and come through a variety of exercises. Once you've got the basics down, you can enter obedience trials and work toward earning your dog's first degree, a C.D. (Companion Dog).

The next level is called "Open," in which jumps and retrieves perk up the dog's interest. Passing grades in competition at this level earn a C.D.X. (Companion Dog Excellent). Beyond that lies the goal of the most ambitious—Utility (U.D. and even U.D.X. or OTCh, an Obedience Champion).

AGILITY

All dogs can participate in the latest canine sport to have gained worldwide popularity for its fun and excitement, agility. It began in England as a canine version of horse show-jumping, but because dogs are more agile and able to perform on verbal commands, extra feats were added such as climbing, balancing and racing through tunnels or in and out of weave poles.

Many of the obstacles (regulation or homemade) can be set up in your own backyard. If the agility bug bites, you could end up in international competition!

For starters, your dog should be obedience trained, even though, in the beginning, the lessons may all be taught on lead. Once the dog understands the commands (and you do, too), it's as easy as guiding the dog over a prescribed course, one obstacle at a time. In competition, the race is against the clock, so wear your running shoes! The dog starts with 200 points and the judge deducts for infractions and misadventures along the way.

All dogs seem to love agility and respond to it as if they were being turned loose in a playground paradise. Your dog's enthusiasm will be contagious; agility turns into great fun for dog and owner.

FIELD TRIALS AND HUNTING TESTS

There are field trials and hunting tests for the sporting breeds—retrievers, spaniels and pointing breeds, and for some hounds—Bassets, Beagles and Dachshunds. Field trials are competitive events that test a dog's ability to perform the functions for which she was bred. Hunting tests, which are open to retrievers,

---

TITLES AWARDED BY THE AKC

Conformation: Ch. (Champion)

Obedience: CD (Companion Dog); CDX (Companion Dog Excellent); UD (Utility Dog); UDX (Utility Dog Excellent); OTCh. (Obedience Trial Champion)

Field: JH (Junior Hunter); SH (Senior Hunter); MH (Master Hunter); AFCh. (Amateur Field Champion); FCh. (Field Champion)

Lure Coursing: JC (Junior Courser); SC (Senior Courser)

Herding: HT (Herding Tested); PT (Pre-Trial Tested); HS (Herding Started); HI (Herding Intermediate); HX (Herding Excellent); HCh. (Herding Champion)

Tracking: TD (Tracking Dog); TDX (Tracking Dog Excellent)

Agility: NAD (Novice Agility); OAD (Open Agility); ADX (Agility Excellent); MAX (Master Agility)

Earthdog Tests: JE (Junior Earthdog); SE (Senior Earthdog); ME (Master Earthdog)

Canine Good Citizen: CGC

Combination: DC (Dual Champion—Ch. and Fch.); TC (Triple Champion—Ch., Fch., and OTCh.)

spaniels and pointing breeds only, are noncompetitive and are a means of judging the dog's ability as well as that of the handler.

Hunting is a very large and complex part of canine sports, and if you own one of the breeds that hunts, the events are a great treat for your dog and you. He gets to do what he was bred for, and you get to work with him and watch him do it. You'll be proud of and amazed at what your dog can do.

Fortunately, the AKC publishes a series of booklets on these events, which outline the rules and regulations and include a glossary of the sometimes complicated terms. The AKC also publishes newsletters for field tri-alers and hunting test enthusiasts. The United Kennel Club (UKC) also has informative materials for the hunter and his dog.

Retrievers and other sporting breeds get to do what they're bred to in hunt-ing tests.

HERDING TESTS AND TRIALS

Herding, like hunting, dates back to the first known uses man made of dogs. The interest in herding today is widespread, and if you own a herding breed, you can join in the activity. Herding dogs are tested for their natural skills to keep a flock of ducks, sheep or cattle together. If your dog shows potential, you can start at the testing level, where your dog can earn a title for showing an inherent herding ability. With training you can advance to the trial level, where your dog should be capable of controlling even diffi-cult livestock in diverse situations.

LURE COURSING

The AKC Tests and Trials for Lure Coursing are open to traditional sighthounds—Greyhounds, Whippets,

Borzoi, Salukis, Afghan Hounds, Ibizan Hounds and Scottish Deerhounds—as well as to Basenjis and Rhodesian Ridgebacks. Hounds are judged on overall ability, follow, speed, agility and endurance. This is possibly the most exciting of the trials for spectators, because the speed and agility of the dogs is awesome to watch as they chase the lure (or "course") in heats of two or three dogs at a time.

TRACKING

Tracking is another activity in which almost any dog can compete because every dog that sniffs the ground when taken outdoors is, in fact, tracking. The hard part comes when the rules as to what, when and where the dog tracks are determined by a person, not the dog! Tracking tests cover a large area of fields, woods and roads. The tracks are laid hours before the dogs go to work on them, and include "tricks" like cross-tracks and sharp turns. If you're interested in search-and-rescue work, this is the place to start.

This tracking dog is hot on the trail.

EARTHDOG TESTS FOR SMALL TERRIERS AND DACHSHUNDS

These tests are open to Australian, Bedlington, Border, Cairn, Dandie Dinmont, Smooth and Wire Fox, Lakeland, Norfolk, Norwich, Scottish, Sealyham, Skye, Welsh and West Highland White Terriers as well as Dachshunds. The dogs need no prior training for this terrier sport. There is a qualifying test on the day of the event, so dog and handler learn the rules on the spot. These tests, or "digs," sometimes end with informal races in the late afternoon.

Here are some of the extracurricular obedience and racing activities that are not regulated by the AKC or UKC, but are generally run by clubs or a group of dog fanciers and are often open to all.

Canine Freestyle This activity is something new on the scene and is variously likened to dancing, dressage or ice skating. It is meant to show the athleticism of the dog, but also requires showmanship on the part of the dog's handler. If you and your dog like to ham it up for friends, you might want to look into freestyle.

Lure coursing lets sighthounds do what they do best—run!

Scent Hurdle Racing Scent hurdle racing is purely a fun activity sponsored by obedience clubs with members forming competing teams. The height of the hurdles is based on the size of the shortest dog on the team. On a signal, one team dog is released on each of two side-by-side courses and must clear every hurdle before picking up its own dumbbell from a platform and returning over the jumps to the handler. As each dog returns, the next on that team is sent. Of course, that is what the dogs are supposed to do. When the dogs improvise (going under or around the hurdles, stealing another dog's dumbbell, and so forth), it no doubt frustrates the handlers, but just adds to the fun for everyone else.

Flyball This type of racing is similar, but after negotiating the four hurdles, the dog comes to a flyball box, steps on a lever that releases a tennis ball into the air, catches the ball and returns over the hurdles to the starting point. This game also becomes extremely fun for spectators because the dogs sometimes cheat by catching a ball released by the dog in the next lane. Three titles can be earned—Flyball Dog (F.D.), Flyball Dog Excellent (F.D.X.) and Flyball Dog Champion (Fb.D.Ch.)—all awarded by the North American Flyball Association, Inc.

Dogsledding The name conjures up the Rocky Mountains or the frigid North, but you can find dogsled clubs in such unlikely spots as Maryland, North Carolina and Virginia! Dogsledding is primarily for the Nordic breeds such as the Alaskan Malamutes, Siberian Huskies and Samoyeds, but other breeds can try. There are some practical backyard applications to this sport, too. With parental supervision, almost any strong dog could pull a child's sled.

Coming over the A-frame on an agility course.

These are just some of the many recreational ways you can get to know and understand your multifaceted dog better and have fun doing it.

10

chapter **10**

Your Dog
and your
Family

by Bardi McLennan

Adding a dog automatically increases your family by one, no matter whether you live alone in an apartment or are part of a mother, father and six kids household. The single-person family is fair game for numerous and varied canine misconceptions as to who is dog and who pays the bills, whereas a dog in a houseful of children will consider himself to be just one of the gang, littermates all. One dog and one child may give a dog reason to believe they are both kids or both dogs. Either interpretation requires parental supervision and sometimes speedy intervention.

As soon as one paw goes through the door into your home, Rufus (or Rufina) has to make many adjustments to become a part of your family. Your job is to make him fit in as painlessly as possible. An older dog may have some frame of reference from past experience, but to a 10-week-old puppy, everything is brand new: people, furniture, stairs, when and where people eat, sleep or watch TV, his own place and everyone else's space, smells, sounds, outdoors—everything!

Puppies, and newly acquired dogs of any age, do not need what we think of as "freedom." If you leave a new dog or puppy loose in the house, you will almost certainly return to chaotic destruction and the dog will forever after equate your homecoming with a time of punishment to be dreaded. It is unfair to give your dog what amounts to "freedom to get into trouble." Instead, confine him to a crate for brief periods of your absence (up to three or four hours) and, for the long haul, a workday for example, confine him to one untrashable area with his own toys, a bowl of water and a radio left on (low) in another room.

Lots of pets get along with each other just fine.

For the first few days, when not confined, put Rufus on a long leash tied to your wrist or waist. This umbilical cord method enables the dog to learn all about you from your body language and voice, and to learn by his own actions which things in the house are NO! and which ones are rewarded by "Good dog." House-training will be easier with the pup always by your side. Speaking of which, accidents do happen. That goal of "completely housetrained" takes up to a year, or the length of time it takes the pup to mature.

The All-Adult Family

Most dogs in an adults-only household today are likely to be latchkey pets, with no one home all day but the dog. When you return after a tough day on the job, the dog can and should be your relaxation therapy. But going home can instead be a daily frustration.

Separation anxiety is a very common problem for the dog in a working household. It may begin with whines and barks of loneliness, but it will soon escalate into a frenzied destruction derby. That is why it is so important to set aside the time to teach a dog to relax when left alone in his confined area and to understand that he can trust you to return.

Let the dog get used to your work schedule in easy stages. Confine him to one room and go in and out of that room over and over again. Be casual about it. No physical, voice or eye contact. When the pup no longer even notices your comings and goings, leave the house for varying lengths of time, returning to stay home for a few minutes and gradually increasing the time away. This training can take days, but the dog is learning that you haven't left him forever and that he can trust you.

Any time you leave the dog, but especially during this training period, be casual about your departure. No anxiety-building fond farewells. Just "Bye" and go! Remember the "Good dog" when you return to find everything more or less as you left it.

If things are a mess (or even a disaster) when you return, greet the dog, take him outside to eliminate, and then put him in his crate while you clean up. Rant and rave in the shower! *Do not* punish the dog. You were not there when it happened, and the rule is: Only punish as you catch the dog in the act of wrongdoing. Obviously, it makes sense to get your latchkey puppy when you'll have a week or two to spend on these training essentials.

Family weekend activities should include Rufus whenever possible. Depending on the pup's age, now is the time for a long walk in the park, playtime in the backyard, a hike in the woods. Socializing is as important as health care, good food and physical exercise, so visiting Aunt Emma or Uncle Harry and the next-door neighbor's dog or cat is essential to developing an out-going, friendly temperament in your pet.

If you are a single adult, socializing Rufus at home and away will prevent him from becoming overly protective of you (or just overly attached) and will also prevent such behavioral problems as dominance or fear of strangers.

Babies

Whether already here or on the way, babies figure larger than life in the eyes of a dog. If the dog is there first, let him in on all your baby preparations in the house. When baby arrives, let Rufus sniff any item of clothing that has been on the baby before Junior comes home. Then let Mom greet the dog first before introducing the new family member. Hold the baby down for the dog to see and sniff, but make sure some-

one's holding the dog on lead in case of any sudden moves. Don't play keep-away or tease the dog with the baby, which only invites undesirable jump-ing up.

The dog and the baby are "family," and for starters can be treated almost as equals. Things rapidly change, however, especially when baby takes to creeping around on all fours on the dog's turf or, better yet, has yummy pudding all over her face and hands! That's when a lot of things in the dog's and baby's lives become more separate than equal.

Dogs are perfect confidants.

Toddlers make terrible dog owners, but if you can't avoid the combination, use patient discipline (that is, positive teaching rather than punishment), and use time-outs before you run out of patience.

A dog and a baby (or toddler, or an assertive young child) should never be left alone together. Take the dog with you or confine him. With a baby or youngsters in the house, you'll have plenty of use for that wonderful canine safety device called a crate!

Young Children

Any dog in a house with kids will behave pretty much as the kids do, good or bad. But even good dogs and good children can get into trouble when play becomes rowdy and active.

Teach children how to play nicely with a puppy.

Legs bobbing up and down, shrill voices screeching, a ball hurtling overhead, all add up to exuberant frustration for a dog who's just trying to be part of the gang. In a pack of puppies, any legs or toys being chased would be caught by a set of teeth, and all the pups involved would understand that is how the game is played. Kids do not understand this, nor do parents tolerate it. Bring Rufus indoors before you have reason to regret it. This is time-out, not a punishment.

You can explain the situation to the children and tell them they must play quieter games until the puppy learns not to grab them with his mouth. Unfortunately, you can't explain it that easily to the dog. With adult supervision, they will learn how to play together.

Young children love to tease. Sticking their faces or wiggling their hands or fingers in the dog's face is teasing. To another person it might be just annoying, but it is threatening to a dog. There's another difference: We can make the child stop by an explanation, but the only way a dog can stop it is with a warning growl and then with teeth. Teasing is the major cause of children being bitten by their pets. Treat it seriously.

140

Older Children

The best age for a child to get a first dog is between the ages of 8 and 12. That's when kids are able to accept some real responsibility for their pet. Even so, take the child's vow of "I will never *ever* forget to feed (brush, walk, etc.) the dog" for what it's worth: a child's good intention at that moment. Most kids today have extra lessons, soccer practice, Little League, ballet, and so forth piled on top of school schedules. There will be many times when Mom will have to come to the dog's rescue. "I walked the dog for you so you can set the table for me" is one way to get around a missed appointment without laying on blame or guilt.

Kids in this age group make excellent obedience trainers because they are into the teaching/learning process themselves and they lack the self-consciousness of adults. Attending a dog show is something the whole family can enjoy, and watching Junior Showmanship may catch the eye of the kids. Older children can begin to get involved in many of the recreational activities that were reviewed in the previous chapter. Some of the agility obstacles, for example, can be set up in the backyard as a family project (with an adult making sure all the equipment is safe and secure for the dog).

Older kids are also beginning to look to the future, and may envision themselves as veterinarians or trainers or show dog handlers or writers of the next Lassie best-seller. Dogs are perfect confidants for these dreams. They won't tell a soul.

Other Pets

Introduce all pets tactfully. In a dog/cat situation, hold the dog, not the cat. Let two dogs meet on neutral turf—a stroll in the park or a walk down the street—with both on loose leads to permit all the normal canine ways of saying hello, including routine sniffing, circling, more sniffing, and so on. Small creatures such as hamsters, chinchillas or mice must be kept safe from their natural predators (dogs and cats).

Festive Family Occasions

Parties are great for people, but not necessarily for puppies. Until all the guests have arrived, put the dog in his crate or in a room where he won't be disturbed. A socialized dog can join the fun later as long as he's not underfoot, annoying guests or into the hors d'oeuvres.

There are a few dangers to consider, too. Doors opening and closing can allow a puppy to slip out unnoticed in the confusion, and you'll be organizing a search party instead of playing host or hostess. Party food and buffet service are not for dogs. Let Rufus party in his crate with a nice big dog biscuit.

At Christmas time, not only are tree decorations dangerous and breakable (and perhaps family heirlooms), but extreme caution should be taken with the lights, cords and outlets for the tree lights and any other festive lighting. Occasionally a dog lifts a leg, ignoring the fact that the tree is indoors. To avoid this, use a canine repellent, made for gardens, on the tree. Or keep him out of the tree room unless supervised. And whatever you do, *don't* invite trouble by hanging his toys on the tree!

Car Travel

Before you plan a vacation by car or RV with Rufus, be sure he enjoys car travel. Nothing spoils a holiday quicker than a carsick dog! Work within the dog's comfort level. Get in the car with the dog in his crate or attached to a canine car safety belt and just sit there until he relaxes. That's all. Next time, get in the car, turn on the engine and go nowhere. Just sit. When that is okay, turn on the engine and go around the block. Now you can go for a ride and include a stop where you get out, leaving the dog for a minute or two.

On a warm day, always park in the shade and leave windows open several inches. And return quickly. It only takes 10 minutes for a car to become an overheated steel death trap.

Motel or Pet Motel?

Not all motels or hotels accept pets, but you have a much better choice today than even a few years ago. To find a dog-friendly lodging, look at *On the Road Again With Man's Best Friend,* a series of directories that detail bed and breakfasts, inns, family resorts and other hotels/motels. Some places require a refundable deposit to cover any damage incurred by the dog. More B&Bs accept pets now, but some restrict the size.

If taking Rufus with you is not feasible, check out boarding kennels in your area. Your veterinarian may offer this service, or recommend a kennel or two he or she is familiar with. Go see the facilities for yourself, ask about exercise, diet, housing, and so on. Or, if you'd rather have Rufus stay home, look into bonded petsitters, many of whom will also bring in the mail and water your plants.

chapter 11

Your Dog
and your
Community

by Bardi McLennan

Step outside your home with your dog and you are no longer just family, you are both part of your community. This is when the phrase "responsible pet ownership" takes on serious implications. For starters, it means you pick up after your dog—not just occasionally, but every time your dog eliminates away from home. That means you have joined the Plastic Baggy Brigade! You always have plastic sandwich bags in your pocket and several in the car. It means you teach your kids how to use them, too. If you think this is "yucky," just imagine what

the person (a non-doggy person) who inadvertently steps in the mess thinks!

Your responsibility extends to your neighbors: To their ears (no annoying barking); to their property (their garbage, their lawn, their flower beds, their cat—especially their cat); to their kids (on bikes, at play); to their kids' toys and sports equipment.

There are numerous dog-related laws, ranging from simple dog licensing and leash laws to those holding you liable for any physical injury or property damage done by your dog. These laws are in place to protect everyone in the community, including you and your dog. There are town ordinances and state laws which are by no means the same in all towns or all states. Ignorance of the law won't get you off the hook. The time to find out what the laws are where you live is now.

Be sure your dog's license is current. This is not just a good local ordinance, it can make the difference between finding your lost dog or not.

Many states now require proof of rabies vaccination and that the dog has been spayed or neutered before issuing a license. At the same time, keep up the dog's annual immunizations.

Dressing your dog up makes him appealing to strangers.

Never let your dog run loose in the neighborhood. This will not only keep you on the right side of the leash law, it's the outdoor version of the rule about not giving your dog "freedom to get into trouble."

Good Canine Citizen

Sometimes it's hard for a dog's owner to assess whether or not the dog is sufficiently socialized to be accepted by the community at large. Does Rufus or Rufina display good, controlled behavior in public? The AKC's Canine Good Citizen program is available through many dog organizations. If your dog passes the test, the title "CGC" is earned.

145

The overall purpose is to turn your dog into a good neighbor and to teach you about your responsibility to your community as a dog owner. Here are the ten things your dog must do willingly:

1. Accept a stranger stopping to chat with you.
2. Sit and be petted by a stranger.
3. Allow a stranger to handle him or her as a groomer or veterinarian would.
4. Walk nicely on a loose lead.
5. Walk calmly through a crowd.
6. Sit and down on command, then stay in a sit or down position while you walk away.
7. Come when called.
8. Casually greet another dog.
9. React confidently to distractions.
10. Accept being left alone with someone other than you and not become overly agitated or nervous.

Schools and Dogs

Schools are getting involved with pet ownership on an educational level. It has been proven that children who are kind to animals are humane in their attitude toward other people as adults.

A dog is a child's best friend, and so children are often primary pet owners, if not the primary caregivers. Unfortunately, they are also the ones most often bitten by dogs. This occurs due to a lack of understanding that pets, no matter how sweet, cuddly and loving, are still animals. Schools, along with parents, dog clubs, dog fanciers and the AKC, are working to change all that with video programs for children not only in grade school, but in the nursery school and pre-kindergarten age group. Teaching youngsters how to be responsible dog owners is important community work. When your dog has a CGC, volunteer to take part in an educational classroom event put on by your dog club.

Boy Scout Merit Badge

A Merit Badge for Dog Care can be earned by any Boy Scout ages 11 to 18. The requirements are not easy, but amount to a complete course in responsible dog care and general ownership. Here are just a few of the things a Scout must do to earn that badge:

Point out ten parts of the dog using the correct names.

Give a report (signed by parent or guardian) on your care of the dog (feeding, food used, housing, exercising, grooming and bathing), plus what has been done to keep the dog healthy.

Explain the right way to obedience train a dog, and demonstrate three comments.

Several of the requirements have to do with health care, including first aid, handling a hurt dog, and the dangers of home treatment for a serious ailment.

The final requirement is to know the local laws and ordinances involving dogs.

There are similar programs for Girl Scouts and 4-H members.

Local Clubs

Local dog clubs are no longer in existence just to put on a yearly dog show. Today, they are apt to be the hub of the community's involvement with pets. Dog clubs conduct educational forums with big-name speakers, stage demonstrations of canine talent in a busy mall and take dogs of various breeds to schools for classroom discussion.

The quickest way to feel accepted as a member in a club is to volunteer your services! Offer to help with something—anything—and watch your popularity (and your interest) grow.

Therapy Dogs

Once your dog has earned that essential CGC and reliably demonstrates a steady, calm temperament, you could look into what therapy dogs are doing in your area.

Therapy dogs go with their owners to visit patients at hospitals or nursing homes, generally remaining on leash but able to coax a pat from a stiffened hand, a smile from a blank face, a few words from sealed lips or a hug from someone in need of love.

Nursing homes cover a wide range of patient care. Some specialize in care of the elderly, some in the treatment of specific illnesses, some in physical therapy. Children's facilities also welcome visits from trained therapy dogs for boosting morale in their pediatric patients. Hospice care for the terminally ill and the at-home care of AIDS patients are other areas where this canine visiting is desperately needed. Therapy dog training comes first.

Your dog can make a difference in lots of lives.

There is a lot more involved than just taking your nice friendly pooch to someone's bedside. Doing therapy dog work involves your own emotional stability as well as that of your dog. But once you have met all the requirements for this work, making the rounds once a week or once a month with your therapy dog is possibly the most rewarding of all community activities.

Disaster Aid

This community service is definitely not for everyone, partly because it is time-consuming. The initial training is rigorous, and there can be no let-up in the continuing workouts, because members are on call 24 hours a day to go wherever they are needed at a moment's notice. But if you think you would like to be able to assist in a disaster, look into search-and-rescue work. The network of search-and-rescue volunteers is worldwide, and all members of the American Rescue Dog Association (ARDA) who are qualified to do this work are volunteers who train and maintain their own dogs.

Physical Aid

Most people are familiar with Seeing Eye dogs, which serve as blind people's eyes, but not with all the other work that dogs are trained to do to assist the disabled. Dogs are also specially trained to pull wheelchairs, carry school books, pick up dropped objects, open and close doors. Some also are ears for the deaf. All these assistance-trained dogs, by the way, are allowed anywhere "No Pet" signs exist (as are therapy dogs when properly identified). Getting started in any of this fascinating work requires a background in dog training and canine behavior, but there are also volunteer jobs ranging from answering the phone to cleaning out kennels to providing a foster home for a puppy. You have only to ask.

Making the rounds with your therapy dog can be very rewarding.

part four

Beyond the Basics

chapter 12

Recommended Reading

Books

GENERAL

American Kennel Club (AKC). *American Kennel Club Dog Care and Training.* New York: Howell Book House, 1991.

————. *The Complete Dog Book,* 19th Edition Revised. New York: Howell Book House, 1998.

Bamberger, Michelle, DVM. *Help! The Quick Guide to First Aid for Your Dog.* New York: Howell Book House, 1995.

Carlson, Liisa, DVM, and James Giffin, MD. *Dog Owners Home Veterinary Handbook,* 3rd Edition. New York: Howell Book House, 1999.

DeBitetto, James, DVM, and Sarah Hodgson. *You & Your Puppy.* New York: Howell Book House, 2000.

Rogers Clark, Anne, and Andrew H. Brace. *The International Encyclopedia of Dogs.* New York: Howell Book House, 1995.

Vella, Bob, and Ken Leebow. *300 Incredible Things for Pet Lovers on the Internet.* Marietta, Georgia: 300 Incredible.com, 2000.

Volhard, Wendy, and Kerry Brown, DVM. *Holistic Guide for a Healthy Dog.* New York: Howell Book House, 2000.

ABOUT DOG SHOWS

Alston, George. *The Winning Edge.* New York: Howell Book House, 1992.

Hall, Lynn. *Dog Showing for Beginners.* New York: Howell Book House, 1994.

About Training

Arden, Andrea. *Dog-Friendly Dog Training.* New York: Howell Book House, 1999.

Benjamin, Carol Lea. *Dog Training for Kids.* New York: Howell Book House, 1988.

————. *Dog Training in 10 Minutes.* New York: Howell Book House, 1997.

Burch, Mary, PhD, and Jon Bailey. *How Dogs Learn.* New York: Howell Book House, 1999.

Dunbar, Ian, PhD, MRCVS. *Dog Behavior: An Owner's Guide to a Happy Healthy Pet.* New York: Howell Book House, 1996.

————. *How to Teach a New Dog Old Tricks.* James & Kenneth Publishers, 1998. Order from the publisher at 2140 Shattuck Ave. #2406, Berkeley, CA 94704. (510) 658-8588.

Evans, Job Michael. *People, Pooches and Problems.* New York: Howell Book House, 2001.

Hodgson, Sarah. *Dogperfect: The User Friendly Guide to a Well Behaved Dog.* New York: Howell Book House, 1995.

New Skete Monks. *How to Be Your Dog's Best Friend.* Boston: Little Brown & Company, 1978.

Pryor, Karen. *Don't Shoot the Dog! The New Art of Teaching and Training,* Revised Edition. New York: Bantam Doubleday Dell, 1999.

Rutherford, Clarice, and David H. Neil, MRCVS. *How to Raise a Puppy You Can Live With.* Loveland, Colorado: Alpine Publications, 1982.

Volhard, Jack, and Melissa Bartlett. *What All Good Dogs Should Know: The Sensible Way to Train.* New York: Howell Book House, 1991.

About Breeding

Finder Harris, Beth J. *Breeding a Litter: The Complete Book of Prenatal and Postnatal Care.* New York: Howell Book House, 1993.

Holst, Phyllis. *Canine Reproduction: The Breeder's Guide.* Loveland, Colorado: Alpine Publications, 1999.

Walkowicz, Chris, and Bonnie Wilcox, DVM. *Successful Dog Breeding: The Complete Handbook of Canine Midwifery.* New York: Howell Book House, 1994.

American Rescue Dog Association. *Search and Rescue Dogs.*
New York: Howell Book House, 1991.

Barwig, Susan, and Stewart Hilliard. *Schutzhund.* New
York: Howell Book House, 1991.

Burch, Mary. *Volunteering with Your Pet.* New York: Howell
Book House, 1996.

O'Neil, Jacqueline F. *All About Agility.* New York: Howell
Book House, 1999.

Vollhard, Jack and Wendy. *The Canine Good Citizen.* New
York: Howell Book House, 1994.

Magazines

The AKC GAZETTE, The Official Journal for the Sport of
Purebred Dogs
American Kennel Club
260 Madison Avenue
New York, NY 10016
(212) 696-8200
www.akc.org

The Bark
2810 8th Street
Berkeley, CA 94710
(510) 704-0827
www.thebark.com

Dog Fancy
Fancy Publications
3 Burroughs
Irvine, CA 92718
(949) 855-8822
www.animalnetwork.com

Dog & Kennel
Pet Publishing, Inc.
7-L Dundas Circle
Greensboro, NC 27407
(336) 292-4047
www.dogandkennel.com

Dog Watch Newsletter
P.O. Box 420235
Palm Coast, FL 32142-0235
(800) 829-5574
www.vet.cornell.edu/publicresources/dog

Dog World
Primedia
500 North Dearborn, Suite 1100
Chicago, IL 60610
(877) 224-7711
www.dogworldmag.com

Videos

"SIRIUS Puppy Training," by Ian Dunbar, PhD, MRCVS. James & Kenneth Publishers, 2140 Shattuck Ave. #2406, Berkeley, CA 94704. Order from the publisher.

"Training the Companion Dog," from Dr. Dunbar's British TV Series, James & Kenneth Publishers. (See address above.)

The American Kennel Club produces videos on every breed of dog, as well as on hunting tests, field trials and other areas of interest to purebred dog owners. For more information, write to AKC/Video Fulfillment, 5580 Centerview Dr., Suite 200, Raleigh, NC 27606. The AKC can be reached at (919) 233-9767, or visit its Web site at www.akc.org.

chapter 13

Resources

Breed Clubs and Registries

Registry organizations register purebred dogs. The American Kennel Club is the oldest and largest in the United States, and currently recognizes over 130 breeds. The United Kennel Club registers some breeds the AKC doesn't (including the American Pit Bull Terrier and the Miniature Fox Terrier), as well as many of the same breeds. The other clubs included here are for your reference; the AKC can provide you with a list of foreign registries.

Every breed recognized by the American Kennel Club has a national (parent) club. National clubs are a great source of information on your breed. You can get the name of the secretary of the club by contacting:

American Kennel Club (AKC)
260 Madison Avenue, 4th Floor
New York, NY 10016
(212) 696-8200
www.akc.org

For breeder referrals, call the customer service department in North Carolina at (919) 233-9767, or visit their Web site.

United Kennel Club (UKC)
100 East Kilgore Road
Portage, MI 49002-5584
(616) 343-9020
www.ukcdogs.com

American Rare Breed Association (ARBA)
9921 Frank Tippet Road
Cheltenham, MD 20612
(301) 868-5718
www.arba.org

155

Canadian Kennel Club (CKC)
89 Skyway Avenue
Etobicoke, Ontario
Canada M9W 6R4
(800) 250-8040
(416) 675-5511
information@ckc.ca

Health Registries

CERF
Department of Veterinary Clinical Science
School of Veterinary Medicine
Purdue University
West Lafayette, IN 47907
(765) 494-8179
yshen@vet.purdue.edu

Orthopedic Foundation for Animals (OFA)
2300 East Nifong Boulevard
Columbia, MO 65201-3856
(573) 442-0418
ofa@ofa.org
(Hip registry)

Activity Clubs

Write to the following organizations for information on the
activities they sponsor.

American Kennel Club (AKC)
260 Madison Avenue, 4th Floor
New York, NY 10016
(212) 696-8200
www.akc.org
(Conformation Shows, Obedience Trials, Field Trials and
Hunting Tests, Agility, Canine Good Citizen, Lure Coursing,
Herding, Tracking, Earthdog Tests, Coonhunting)

United Kennel Club (UKC)
100 East Kilgore Road
Portage, MI 49002-5584
(616) 343-9020
www.ukcdogs.com
(Conformation Shows, Obedience Trials, Agility, Hunting
for Various Breeds, Terrier Trials and more)

North American Flyball Association
1400 West Devon Avenue, #152
Chicago, IL 60660
www.flyball.org

Trainers

Association of Pet Dog Trainers
66 Morris Avenue, Suite 2A
Springfield, NJ 07081
(800) PET-DOGS
www.apdp.com

National Association of Dog Obedience Instructors
2286 East Steel Road
St. Johns, MI 48879
www.nadoi.org

Dog Friendly Web Sites

The following Web sites offer a variety of experiences for the dog-loving Internet surfer. Some sites present specific breed information, while others provide quizzes and question-naires to help you decide which dog breed is the best one for you and your family. You can view photographs, research breeders and rescue organizations in your area, find out the best ways to exercise or travel with your pet or just discover more about *canis familiaris*. Enjoy!

Dog Breed Information Center
www.dogbreedinfo.com
This is a well-designed site with cute doggie graphics and easy-to-use links. Log on to donate toys to rescue organiza-tions, post messages for like-minded dog folk, take question-naires to discover which dog breed is best suited to your family and your home, view a plethora of canine photographs or discover the answers to frequently asked dog-care and -training questions.

Choosing the Perfect Dog
www.choosingtheperfectdog.net
Another good, all-purpose site for dog owners or dog-owner wannabes. Information is presented in a very organized man-ner, with helpful sidebars and links. Practical answers are given to questions such as "How do I match a dog to my lifestyle?" Or "How much time/money/stuff do I need to provide for a dog?" The site prompts visitors to think carefully about getting a dog, and to responsibly research dog breeds so that everyone involved lives happily ever after.

Good News for Pets
www.goodnewsforpets.com
This weekly digest provides interesting tidbits on all things canine related. It profiles people who are active in the dog community, provides nutrition facts, addresses legal issues

and focuses attention on how dogs are portrayed in books and on film. Visit every Monday for the "Pet Question of the Week."

Dog Advisors
www.dogadvisors.com
This is a fun site where the fancier can delve a little deeper and learn a little more about his or her favorite dog breeds. Different breeds are highlighted at various times, as are specific breeders.

United States Dog Agility Association, Inc. (USDAA)
www.usdaa.com
This USDAA is an international site that gives visitors the opportunity to find out the latest news in the world of agility training. It provides an events calendar, records titles and tournaments, defines performance standards and lists affiliated groups. "Front Page News" is updated on a weekly basis.

Canine Freestyle Federation, Inc.
www.canine-freestyle.org
Welcome to the world of Canine Freestyle—or doggie dancing, if you will. Canine freestyle is performed by dog and trainer in a ring, and all moves are choreographed to music. To learn more, visit this well-designed, comprehensive Web site. The CFF also maintains records of freestyle events and publishes a newsletter.

Pets Welcome
www.petswelcome.com
If you plan on travelling with your pet, a visit to this site is a must. The listings page offers information on over 25,000 hotels, bed & breakfasts, ski resorts, campgrounds and pet-friendly beaches. Plenty of advice and knowledge are provided for those who can't imagine leaving their pet at home.

Vet Info.com
www.vetinfo.com
If your dog is suffering from a particular ailment, you can find out more about it by visiting vetinfo.com. The format of this site is easy to use, with each disease listed in alphabetical order. To delve even deeper into your pet's health, you might subscribe to *Vetinfo Digest* for its "Ask Dr. Mike" Segment.